**Praise for Brian McDonald and *Inv***

"Writing stories is hard. They are stubborn by nature. No matter how many times you master one, the next story is obligated to conceal its faults with an entirely new disguise. Your only recourse is to keep writing, while concurrently increasing your understanding of this deceivingly simple, yet highly complex, organism we call story. Brian McDonald's insightful book does just that. Somehow, Brian has found yet another fresh and objective way to analyze how great stories function, and emboldens you to face the challenge of scaling whatever story mountain looms before you. If I manage to reach the summit of my next story it will be in no small part due to having read *Invisible Ink*."

> —Andrew Stanton (cowriter *Toy Story*,
> *Toy Story 2, A Bug's Life, Monsters, Inc.,*
> and cowriter/director *Finding Nemo* and
> *WALL-E*)

"*Invisible Ink* is a powerful tool for anyone who wants to become a better screenwriter. With elegance and precision, Brian McDonald uses his deep understanding of story and character to pass on essential truths about dramatic writing. Ignore him at your peril."

> —Jim Taylor (Academy Award™-
> winning screenwriter of *Sideways*
> and *Election*)

"Brian McDonald knows that underneath a good story are the difficult mechanics of plot. He offers insights into both the construction needed and the art of hiding that construction."

> —Jim Uhls (screenwriter of *Fight Club*)

*Invisible Ink* is an uncommonly good guidebook that reveals the unseen workings within great movies, TV, and literature. Brian McDonald, the author of the guidebook, is like a modern day magician who understands the enchantment that lives within a good story, and fortunately for us, he is ready to share his many secrets.

—Joel Hodgson (creator of *Mystery Science Theater 3000* and *Cinematic Titanic*)

"Storytelling has been my bread and butter for twenty-five years now, and in that time I've sat down with at least a couple of dozen books that swore they could help me with my craft. *Invisible Ink* is the first one I've finished. Brian McDonald understands story like no one else, from the need for and nature of an underlying structure—'armature' is his fine and nimble term for it—through the land mine-laden path to fleshing it out. McDonald himself is a screenwriter, but this is by no means a book solely for screenwriters. It's not about screenwriting; it's about writing and telling stories. If you're a writer of any kind—fiction, short stories, textbooks, travel articles, newspaper features, you name it—you'll come away from *Invisible Ink* with a deeper grasp of how you do what you do… and how to do it better. And you'll never look at *The Wizard of Oz* in quite the same way again."

—Aaron Elkins
(Edgar Award-winning mystery novelist)

Brian McDonald's *Invisible Ink* lays the foundations for storytellers of any kind to do what they are supposed to do; communicate clearly and entertain. Had I not had the good fortune of meeting Brian when I was young, I have no doubt that I would be aimlessly lost in the miasma of ideas, instead of where I am today.

—Brian Kalin O'Connell (episodic director on the animated *Star Wars: Clone Wars*)

"The nuts and bolts of storytelling are laid out with clarity, passion, and fun. A lively read, with vivid examples throughout. It's inspiring."
—Paul Chadwick (creator of the critically acclaimed comic book, *Concrete*)

"Don't tell anyone, but the secret to exceptional story crafting is written in *Invisible Ink*. I advise you read it, memorize it, and then eat the pages one at a time and digest it thoroughly, so that it stays with you. Besides, you can't afford for this book to fall into the hands of your competitors. Brian's powerful concept of armature as understructure will change the way you look at movies and writing forever."
—Pat Hazell (producer/playwright/ former writer for NBC's *Seinfeld*)

"*Invisible Ink* fell into my hands at just the right time—as I was banging my head against the wall trying to structure a screenplay that had too much going on in it. The book's thoughtful exploration of what makes movies work helped me see my core story clearly, and throw away a third of my material—which I now understand will not be missed. I have a stronger, more focused script thanks to a process inspired by this book."
—George Wing (screenwriter of *50 First Dates*)

"*Invisible Ink* is a great, easy-to-understand, guide to the screenplay writing process. Brian breaks it all down to its simplest form. I found the information the most accessible of any book of this genre. Read it before you start your next script, then read it again when you've finished your first draft.
—Joel Madison (television and film writer/producer)

# Foreword

This is the only book on screenplay structure I have ever had the least inclination to read all the way through. Something has always kept me out of structure books: They seemed too confident to reach for and very unpleasant if you got there. Any semblance of structure in my screenplays has been mainly accidental, relying on emotional tides that often beguiled then drowned me. I love *Invisible Ink* for inviting me in, for showing me I can touch the stove without burning my hand, and for not holding up to me, as examples to follow, more than one of those overwhelmingly intimidating models, the "3 Cs": *Citizen Kane, Chinatown,* and *Casablanca*. Brian McDonald's rich curiosity takes him to different allusions, unexpected literary originals that anyone of courage who had a childhood can climb. Eerily and precisely to the point, they enroll us without threat, not just because they're entertaining in themselves, but because his examples let us hold out our aprons safely to all the trees he plucks them from as we walk with him on the guided tour of his wonderful varied orchard—here Aesop, there nursery rhymes, farther on fairy tales, comic books, cartoons, the Bible, the theater, anthropological discoveries, barroom jokes, Billy Wilder, Shakespeare, Spielberg, Pixar, *The Wizard of Oz*, ancient African proverbs, and two irreplaceables, Joe Guppy, and Matt Smith. With *Invisible Ink* Brian McDonald has written us a book to keep and heed forever because through the simple, graceful, graspable, original wisdom of it, we might just save our screenwriting lives.

Stewart Stern (screenwriter of *Rebel Without a Cause)*

Libertary Edition | Seattle, WA | 2010
Copyright © 2003-2005 Brian McDonald
www.Libertary.com
Second Printing

ISBN 978-0-9841786-2-9

DISCOUNTS OR CUSTOMIZED EDITIONS MAY BE AVAILABLE FOR
EDUCATIONAL AND OTHER GROUPS BASED ON BULK PURCHASE.
For further information please contact info@libertary.com

# INVISIBLE INK

A practical guide to building stories that resonate

By

Brian McDonald

Libertary Editions (Seattle, WA) 2010

## Acknowledgments

I would very much like to thank my former student Heather for insisting that I write this book. And thanks, also, to Pat who convinced me that I could write this book. And thanks very much to Michael who has been a fan of the book since before it existed. And gratitude to Wayno for always being a cheerleader.

All teachers who write books thank their students and I am no different. My students have taught me more about my craft than any teacher ever could.

Thanks too to my family for celebrating all of our triumphs great and small.

And thanks most of all to Heather (my Heather) for sticking through the rough times.

For Scott Tolson,

A friend, a brother, a teacher, and a storyteller.

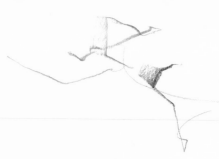

*If you put a gun onstage in Act I you must use it by Act III.*
—Anton Chekhov


*If there is something wrong with the third act, it's really in the first act.*
—Billy Wilder

# TABLE of CONTENTS

| Chapter I |

**What is invisible ink?**

# What is invisible ink?

*"There is no art which does not conceal a still greater art."* – Percival Wilde

A friend of mine once took an anthropology class in which she heard this story: An anthropologist was living among tribal people with little to no contact with the modern world. Wanting to share the marvels of technology with these isolated folks, the anthropologist took a photo of the chief and his wives. When the picture was processed and shown to the chief he was unable to recognize the blotches of black, white, and gray as an image of himself. He had never learned to translate two-dimensional images into recognizable three-dimensional shapes. That same chief, however, could look at a patch of grass and say what kind of animal had traversed it and how long ago with no more difficulty than you or I would have recognizing ourselves in a photographic image.

Story structure works very much this way. It is easy to see if you know what to look for, and invisible to those who don't.

Often when I listen to how people evaluate stories, I hear them talk about dialogue. When they talk about "the script" for a film, they are often talking about the dialogue. Or when they mention how well a book is written, they most often mean the way the words are put together—the beauty of a sentence.

When people speak of Shakespeare's work, they almost always talk about the beauty of the language.

These are all forms of "visible ink." This term refers to writing that is readily "seen" by the reader or viewer, who often mistakes these words on the page as the only writing the storyteller is doing.

But how events in a story are ordered is also writing. What events should occur in a story to make the teller's point is also writing. Why a character behaves in a particular way is also writing.

These are all forms of "invisible ink," so called because they are not easily spotted by a reader, viewer, or listener of a story. Invisible ink does, however, have a profound impact on a story. More to the point, it is the story. Invisible ink is the writing below the surface of the words. Most people will never see or notice it, but they will feel it. If you learn to use it, your work will feel polished, professional, and it will have a profound impact on your audience.

This book teaches you to see the elements that actually constitute story and how to apply them to your own work. Even stories that you are most familiar with will reveal their inner workings to you in ways you have never seen before.

By the end of this book, you will be able to see footprints in the grass.

| Chapter II |

Seven easy steps to a better story

Once upon a time ...

And every day ...

Until one day ...

And because of this ...

And because of this ...

Until finally ...

And ever since that day ...

## Seven easy steps to a better story

Stories are not complicated. They are, in fact, deceptively simple. But like anything simple, they are difficult to create. I realize that sounds a little like Lewis Carroll, but hear me out.

One of the things that hangs us all up when writing is that we feel we need to make it more complicated. We feel that this will make it better, but it never does. It just makes it muddy.

I often hear people say, "less is more." But I don't see it reflected in their work. What follows are seven steps that make up all narratives. I was taught them by a writer/teacher by the name of Matt Smith. He learned them from a guy named Joe Guppy. And you are learning them from me.

**The steps**

1.) Once upon a time _____

2.) And every day _____

3.) Until one day _____

4.) And because of this _____

5.) And because of this _____

6.) Until finally _____

7.) And ever since that day _____

These steps are a kind of invisible ink. I'm sure you recognize them. They just make sense, don't they? Why didn't you know them already? You did. You just thought it would be more complicated than that.

## Once upon a time ...

There are many books you can read that explain three-act structure, so I will cover it only briefly here using the seven steps as a template.

Let's look at the first two steps: Once upon a time and And every day. They are your act 1. What is the purpose of act 1? It tells the audience everything they need to know to understand the story that is to follow.

Let's look at what legendary filmmaker Billy Wilder says about the importance of a good first act: "If there is something wrong with the third act, it's really in the first act." Most of us have no problem understanding the importance of the first act of a joke. When someone tells a joke poorly it is more likely than not that they have forgotten to convey an important piece of information in the set up that makes the punch line funny. So it seems the joke is in the set up and not the punch line.

Just as with a joke, a story's set up must tell the audience everything they need to know to understand the story.

What does an audience need to know? Think of your childhood storybooks: Once upon a time there were Three Bears who lived together in their own house in the forest. Mama Bear, Papa Bear, and Baby Bear. They each had a bowl for their porridge—a small bowl for Baby Bear, a middle-sized bowl for Mama Bear, and a big bowl for Papa Bear.

We know several things just from those few sentences. Yes, we know there are three bears. We know that there are at least three major characters and we know their relationship to one another. But we also know that these bears behave as people. That is important. You could very well have a story where the bears act as animals.

Remember, when you create a story, you must let the audience know the reality of your story. It's your world.

"A duck walks into a bar and orders a rum and Coke." That joke starts by giving you a major character and letting you know the reality. Notice that when a joke starts with a duck walking into a bar, no one says, "That's ridiculous!" They accept it because it's the first thing they are told. Whatever your "talking duck" is, let people know right away.

The opening of *Raiders of the Lost Ark* is often talked about because it's exciting. But it is much more than that. With so many fantastical things happening right at the story's opening, the audience knows a few things about its world. We know that the story's reality is heightened—that it is not to be a story about a soldier coping with his life after Vietnam. It is a fantasy that takes place in the year 1936. We know that in this world, archaeology is much more than just digging for pieces of clay pots. We know, also, that the guy in the fedora is good with a whip and good at his job. He appears to be fearless and smart. Things don't always go as planned for him, and he sometimes survives by the skin of his teeth.

We meet Belloq, Indiana Jones's arch enemy, so we know his is a ruthless business, and men will kill for the valuable artifacts they seek.

We see that Indiana Jones does have his fears: snakes. He's not superhuman.

Which brings up something else. We know some things because they are defined by their absence. We know that Indiana Jones may be skilled, but he does not possess magical powers. In some realities, magical powers are commonplace, but not in this one. There is another Spielberg film that shows what a disaster it can be to have a poor first act: In the mid-1980s, Steven Spielberg produced a television show called *Amazing Stories*. A particular episode, "The Mission," was one Mr. Spielberg also directed.

The story takes place during WWII, aboard a B-17 bomber. B-17s had a crew of ten. One of the crewmen was positioned under the belly of the plane in a Plexiglass bubble so he could fire his machine gun at any threat coming from underneath the plane.

In this story, the "belly-gunner," as they were called, is a talented and likable guy who draws caricatures of his crewmates, much to their amusement. He wants to work for Walt Disney Studios.

The plane goes on a bombing mission and is badly damaged. When the belly-gunner tries to crawl out of his bubble and into the plane, he finds that he is trapped underneath the plane because of the damage.

The crew tries to get him out, but can't. No problem; they can just get him out when they land. Then someone suggests that they check the landing gear—and it doesn't work. Without wheels, the plane will have to land on its belly, crushing the helpless gunner to death.

The crew does not want to give up on their buddy and increases the effort to save him. Nothing works.

Sure that the man will die, the airbase calls a priest to be there when the plane lands.

It becomes painfully clear that the gunner is going to die and there is nothing to be done. Each of the crewmembers puts his hand down the small top opening of the bubble to say his good-byes. They are in tears as they rub the gunner's head or embrace his hand.

Without the belly-gunner's knowledge, the decision has been made to shoot him so that he won't suffer the pain of being crushed.

Slowly, one of the men pulls his pistol and lowers it down to the head of his unsuspecting friend.

The poor gunner is crying and muttering that he can't die because he's going to work for Walt Disney Studios.

The pistol creeps ever closer to his head as he busily sketches a cartoon version of a B-17. He is almost in a trance. He draws big, cartoonish wheels on the bottom of the plane.

As they approach the landing strip, the pilot decides to try one last time to lower the landing gear. His indicators tell him that the wheels have lowered.

From the bottom of the real plane, big exaggerated cartoon tires emerge. They make the sound of a squeaky balloon and are complete with a cartoon tire patch. The plane is able to land on these cartoon tires and the man is saved.

The night this show aired, I had a group of friends over to watch the show. I can tell you that we were riveted to the screen during this show. We kept wondering how the hell they were going to get out of this. The tension and suspense were palpable.

We all reacted with disappointed laughter upon the landing of the plane on cartoon wheels. So, it turns out, did the rest of America.

I can't tell you how disappointed audiences were when this episode aired. I remember how, the next day, people at work talked about how bad it was. They thought the entire episode was awful.

Spielberg had not set up a reality where cartoon tires could save the day. There are realities in which this may be possible: *Who Framed Roger Rabbit*, for example.

Spielberg had done such a good job with the first part of the story that we, the audience, believed the situation was dire. We were invested in the story and its world. The cartoon tires were from some other world we knew nothing about.

Just as Billy Wilder said, "If there is something wrong with the third act, it's really in the first act," so your "Once upon a time" is the reality in which your story takes place and the introduction of your major characters.

"And every day…" just supports what has already been set up. It establishes a pattern. A pattern to be broken by…

## Until one day...

An inciting incident occurs. The inciting incident is the true beginning of your story. If your story is about a couple who has an affair, this might be when they meet. Or if they have already met, it is when the affair begins.

Some will tell you that this is where your conflict begins, but not necessarily. Comic-book writer and editor Jim Shooter has observed that the second act can start with conflict or opportunity. For instance, if you've got a story where the first act is about a young woman who is so poor she can't pay her rent, the first act might end when she finds one million dollars.

This step has been called many things: *act break, plot point, turning point,* and *curtain.* I prefer curtain. The reason I like the term curtain is because it comes from theater, wherein a curtain is literally dropped between acts. In live theater, they must get the audience back after intermission, so acts end on the highest point, when the stakes are at their most desperate. For me, imagining that there is a physical curtain helps me to remember to raise the stakes.

In his book, *Comedy Writing Step by Step,* comedy writer Gene Perret calls this the "Uh-oh factor." In a well-constructed sketch, the character and/or situation is established and then something happens that requires a reaction. He uses an example from the old *Carol Burnett Show* in which Carol plays a woman who has just been released from a hospital psych ward for being addicted to soap operas. She proclaims that she is cured. She says, "I don't care if Bruce marries Wanda or not." Her friend's response is, "Bruce is dead." As Mr. Perret describes it, Carol's eyes widen at this news and the audience thinks, *Uh-oh, she's hooked on soaps again.*

Drama has this uh-oh moment as well. In Shakespeare's *King Lear,* the king promises his entire fortune to the one of his three daughters who can prove she loves him most. That's an uh-oh moment if there ever was one.

Few people could stop watching a drama after something like that is introduced.

**And because of this...**

This is now your second act. When your first "curtain" goes down, that is the end of your first act. Now it is time to explore what happens as a result of your first act—everything should be cause-and-effect. If your character was diagnosed with inoperable cancer at the end of act 1, this is where he deals with it. Does he go into denial? Does he give up, lie down, and wait to die? Or is he a fighter? Will he try anything for another few days of life? Does he question how he has lived his life and try to do something worthwhile before he dies?

Whatever the character does, it must be in reaction to the incident at the act 1 curtain.

**And because of this...**

Act 2 is your longest act and makes up the body of your story. This act is usually split in two. I like to call this split the fulcrum. Because act 2 is so long, it can be difficult to keep an audience engrossed. It helps to cut it in half.

In Billy Wilder's classic noir film, *Double Indemnity*, a woman and her lover decide to kill the woman's husband for the insurance money. In the first half of act 2 they plan the murder. At the fulcrum, they carry out their plan and in the second half of act 2 the focus becomes: Will they get away with this crime?

Back to our character diagnosed with cancer. Let's say that when given the news of his cancer, he gives up on life and begins alienating those who care for him. But at the fulcrum something happens that makes him want to live. Now he will stop at nothing to find a cure.

**Until finally...**

This is your third act. When the third act curtain "goes up," it is the beginning of the end of the story. In a cop drama, for instance, it might be the clue that solves the big mystery and puts the detective on the trail of the killer. This event, whatever it is, starts the chain of events that leads to your climax.

Using our example of the cancer patient, perhaps this is where he makes peace with the inevitable and accepts his impending death. Perhaps he decides to cherish the moments he has left with family and friends and spends his time with them instead of searching for the elusive cure for his disease.

**And ever since that day...**

Following your climax is a short scene or two called a denouement. "They lived happily ever after" is the most familiar denouement. You shouldn't have too much following your climax, just something that lets the audience know what the life of your protagonist is like after it.

In the case of our unfortunate cancer patient, he does not survive; but maybe this is where we see how his courage in the face of death has had a lasting impact on those who survive. Or maybe how he lives on through his art. Or perhaps this death has ended old rivalries and caused others to cherish those around them.

What I would like you to do now is write down each of these steps, followed by a blank space. Then I want you to write a few simple stories using these steps. Make them as simple as possible.

What you will find is that what you have written feels like a story, but seems to lack something. They are shallow for some reason. Forgettable. It is a small matter to fix; all you need to do is have a point.

| Chapter III |


The armature

Joke exercise

What it means to dramatize an idea

"Bundle of sticks"

Theme beats logic

The use of clones

## The armature

*A wise man speaks because he has* something *to say; a fool because he has to say* something.
—Unknown author; often attributed to Plato

Why do people tell stories? The stories that tend to stick to our bones are those that teach us something. This, I believe, is the primary reason we tell stories—to teach.

Consider this: Every culture on the globe has music and stories. We all have music and we all have stories.

People who study human speech believe that humans did not invent language anymore than birds invented flight. It is in our makeup to speak. It is part of being human.

It makes sense to me that stories fall under this category. They are part of us. I've seen memory experts on television who will give volunteers a huge list of objects to memorize. Of course, this is difficult to do. Then they tell the volunteer to string the objects together in an absurd story. When this is done, the list is easily recalled. Our brains seem to retain information this way.

I have read about aboriginal tribes in Australia who use songs and stories in case they get lost. These songs contain information like a map. So if you know the words to a particular song, you can, for instance, find water in an unfamiliar area because you know the song for that area. Besides saving lives, stories can also tell us how we should live.

In Africa, they used to tell the story of a black slave-catcher who helped the English capture his own countrymen and sell them into a life of slavery. One night, after a particularly good catch, the black slave-catcher was celebrating with the English and they all got drunk on rum. The black man passed out, and when he awoke the next day, he found himself in the belly of a slave ship chained to the very people he helped enslave.

This is a cautionary tale that teaches its listener that there is a price to be paid for betrayal.

In Bruno Bettelheim's book, *The Uses of Enchantment: The Meaning and Importance of Fairy Tales*, he tells of the traditional Hindi medical practice of giving the patient a story to contemplate. Through this story the patient would learn from the hero's failures and victories how to deal with and resolve his/her own problem.

This may sound like a foreign concept, but we use this even today in Western culture in the form of Alcoholics Anonymous and other twelve-step programs where people share their stories in order to help themselves and others. This simple act of sharing stories helps the healing process. People learn that they are not alone in their struggle and that others have been through these addictions and survived. They may also learn things to watch out for in their own behavior to avoid falling back into old destructive patterns. Stories teach us how to live.

Take the story of King Midas. This man was so greedy that he wished all he touched would turn to gold. That is until he touched his beloved daughter and she was changed to gold. We learn that some things are more important than money. Like the aboriginal song, this story is a map—a map for living.

Look at the Bible. It could be just a list of rules, but it's not—it's stories. Stories resonate with people. Lists do not.

If you want people to hold fast to their faith no matter what, you tell them the story of Job. Job would not renounce God no matter what the Devil did to him, and in the end he was rewarded.

If you want people to stand up to power, no matter what the odds, tell them the story of David and Goliath.

If you want to teach people not to get too full of themselves, you tell them the story of King Nimrod, who thought himself so great that he tried to build a tower to God. He was put in his place when God gave all the workers different languages so they could not communicate.

The Greeks and Romans had similar stories. All religions have understood, for a very long time, that stories are powerful tools. Why is it that some stories stick with us, while others are soon forgotten? Do you remember the story I told you about the tribal chief and the anthropologist? Sure you do. Why? It's because I had a point, a reason to tell that story. Having a point gives your stories resonance. Recall the saying, "A wise man speaks because he has something to say; a fool because he has to say something." This is true when one is crafting a story as well.

Because of my work at make-up effects houses, I've known a few sculptors. When they begin sculpting in clay, they first build an armature to act as a skeleton; otherwise, the piece would not hold its shape. It might look good for a while but would soon collapse. When an admirer of art looks at a sculpture, she never sees or even thinks about the armature that gives the piece its structural integrity. The armature is invisible but as much a part of the sculpture as the outside.

Before you begin writing, you too must build an armature. For us story-crafters, the armature is the idea upon which we hang our story. It is what has been called theme, but I find that the word theme is not descriptive enough and leads to confusion; I have found in teaching that many people bring a lot of baggage to the table when I address theme.

What is an armature, then, when talking about story craft? It is what you want to say with your piece. I was once talking to a friend who was complaining about a producer wanting to change a scene in his script. My friend was angry because the change had nothing to do with his theme. He said, "My theme is competition. And the change has nothing to do with competition!" I didn't say anything at the time, but my friend was confused. There is an old joke about marriage that goes, "Marriage is not a word, it's a sentence." It's the same with theme. My friend had nothing to say about competition. "Competition" is not a theme. A theme (or armature) might be, "Competition is sometimes a necessary evil." Or, "Competition leads to self-destruction." Saying that your theme is competition is like saying your theme is "red." It really says nothing at all.

One way to look at your armature is what is called, in children's fables, "the moral." The armature is your point. Your story is sculpted around this point.

With King Midas, the storyteller wanted to teach people that some things were more important than money. What were his tasks as a writer? First, he had to create a character who was greedy. Then he needed to set up a situation wherein the character gets what he wants. Then he needed to turn this wish into something that would teach the character a lesson. Everything in this story is designed to make the writer's point. This should be true of your work as well.

Some of you may think this definition of theme too simplistic. *It must be harder than this*, you think. It isn't. You are also worried about being perceived as too preachy. Over the years, I have encountered many students concerned with being too preachy or blatant, but never one who was afraid of not being clear enough or that their point would not be understood.

The first thing you must do to get your point across is to understand what you want to say. I know that sounds simple and obvious, but I almost never meet writers who know what they want to say. Mostly what they want is to say something deep and profound that no one has ever said before, but they don't know what that is. Or they want to say a thousand things in one story, not realizing that to say too much is to say nothing at all.

I was once reading an interview with animation director Chuck Jones in which he talked about animating young animals versus old animals. He had observed that a puppy, for instance, would expend excess energy to perform simple tasks. This results in those floppy movements we associate with young mammals. In contrast, adult animals are more economical. Think of the clumsy hunting style of a kitten versus the precision of an adult cat. I have noticed this same thing with story crafters. Writers with the least experience and skill think that the more complicated something is, the better. But like a kitten their work comes off clumsy and unfocused. If you want to come off like a mature writer, be precise.

There is an old piece of advice usually given to someone about to give a speech: Tell them what you're going to tell them. Tell them. Tell them what you told them. This is no different for storytellers. In fact, those three bits of advice could represent the three acts. But just how do you put this into practice? How is your armature put together?

First, you must know where you are going or you will never get there. Then you must let the audience know where you are taking them. You show them the armature—the idea you want to build on. One way this is done is to have a character state out loud what you want to say with your story.

In *E.T.: The Extra-Terrestrial*, when Elliot says something hurtful to his mother, Elliot's older brother gets angry at his insensitivity and yells, "Damn it, when are you going to grow up and learn how other people feel for a change?" What happens next is that Elliot meets E.T. And one of the first things that happens is that when E.T. becomes sleepy, so does Elliot. Then when E.T. is hungry, so is Elliot. When E.T. drinks beer Elliot gets drunk, too.

Later, when Elliot introduces E.T. to his brother, he says, "I'm keeping him." This without any regard for what E.T. wants. But he is beginning to empathize with others, as is evidenced in the scene in which Elliot feels for the frogs in his science class, and sets them free before they can be dissected. By the end of the film, Elliot "feels what other people feel," enough to send E.T. home even though he will miss his friend. Everything in the film is built on the armature stated by Elliot's brother at the beginning of the story.

*The Iron Giant* is an amazing animated film directed by Brad Bird. On its surface, this film is like E.T. in many ways. It is about a boy who befriends a being from outer space (in this case, a giant robot). And, as in E.T., the government is seeking the alien. So what's different about it, you might ask. It's the armature. As a matter of fact, I heard very few people compare the two films. They each had something different to say, so the similar stuff on the surface didn't matter much.

In the story of *The Iron Giant*, the robot is damaged when it gets to earth. Later, after befriending the boy, the kindly robot remembers that it is programmed to be a weapon of mass destruction. In fact, it nearly vaporizes the boy by accident. Now, the robot has an internal conflict. Will it give in to its programming (its nature) or rise above it? I understand, when Mr. Bird pitched the story, he said, "What if a gun had a conscience and didn't want to be a gun anymore?" That was his armature. In the film it is stated this way: "You are who you choose to be."

The success of *There's Something About Mary* sent Hollywood rushing to produce toilet-humor comedies. But the Farelly brothers had made other shock comedies, why did this one become a megahit that almost everyone seemed to love? I thought the film was so good I saw it three times in the theater. If you knew me, you'd know that I like few films. And I certainly don't like sophomoric humor. So again, why this film? It had an armature.

I don't believe that audiences care much about the genre of a story; they just want to be moved in some way. And they respond over and over again to stories with an armature.

In *There's Something About Mary*, Ben Stiller's character is dishonest to Mary and to himself. He is a stalker, and until he realizes it, he is not worthy of Mary's love.

A film like James Cameron's *Terminator* would seem, on its surface, to have a flimsy armature, but it really has something meaningful to say. If you recall, Sarah Conner was an ordinary 20th-century woman with a stressful low-wage job at a burger joint. In the first act of the film, Sarah is having a particularly bad day at work when her coworker says to her, "Look at it this way, in a hundred years, who will care?"

As it turns out, Sarah's life is about to be turned upside down. A robot from the future has been sent back in time to kill her, to prevent her from giving birth to her son, who is a threat to Skynet (the computer that rules the future earth). She is, according to the film, one of the most important people ever born. So this mundane life that she lives does, indeed, matter. In a hundred years, everyone will care who Sarah Connor was.

This is not unlike *It's a Wonderful Life*, wherein George Bailey thinks it would make little difference to the world if he had never been born. He learns, of course, that his life has had a great impact on those people around him, and even on some he has never met.

These two movies would, on the surface, seem to have nothing in common, but they share a common armature: none of us knows how important our mundane lives may prove to be.

Yes, these are all high-key fantasy films, but armature also applies to straight dramas. They can also state their armature out loud. In *Kramer vs. Kramer*, a story in which Dustin Hoffman's wife, played by Meryl Streep, walks out on him and leaves him with their child, Dustin is speaking with a neighbor who tells him that what Meryl did took a lot of courage. His response is: "Oh, yeah, how much courage does it take to walk out on your child?" By the end of the film, that question is answered for Dustin and for the audience. Watch it and see.

In the *The Wizard of Oz* the armature is stated: "There's no place like home." But it might more accurately be said: "You may already have what you are looking for." How do we know that this is so? Is it because it is said? No, it's because it is dramatized.

Remember that your armature is the foundation that holds up your story. Everything hangs on top of it. Every decision you make should be based on the idea of dramatizing your armature idea.

## Joke exercise

I like to use jokes as an instructional tool because they are short stories of a type and are great for teaching structure. One can learn much about invisible ink from the study of jokes. Just as all elements of a joke support the punch line, so should every element of your story support its armature. Good story structure means that nothing is extraneous; every element leads to an inevitable, yet surprising, conclusion.

Choose the appropriate punch lines for the following jokes.

### Joke Number One:

*A seaman meets a pirate in a bar. The two men take turns boasting of their adventures on the high seas.*

*The seaman notes the pirate has a peg leg, hook, and an eyepatch. He asks, "So how did you end up with the pegleg?"*

*The pirate replies, "We were in a storm at sea, and I was swept overboard into a school of sharks. Just as my men were pulling me out, a shark bit my leg off."*

*"Wow!" said the seaman. "What about your hook?"*

*"Well," replied the pirate, "while my men and I were plundering in the Middle East, I was caught stealing from a merchant. I was arrested and my hand was cut off."*

*"Incredible!" remarked the seaman. "How did you get the eyepatch?"*

*"A sea gull dropping fell into my eye," replied the pirate.*

*"You lost your eye to a sea gull dropping?" the sailor asked incredulously. "Incredible!" remarked the seaman.*

*"Well," said the pirate,*

A.) **"In a pig's eye!"**
B.) **"I've seen bigger."**
C.) **"It was my first day with the hook ..."**
D.) **"I'm thinking, I'm thinking!"**

**Joke Number Two:**
*A guy goes into a bar, orders twelve shots of their finest Scotch whiskey, and starts drinking them as fast as he can.*
*The bartender says, "Dang, why are you drinking so fast?"*
*The guy says, "You would be drinking fast if you had what I had."*
*The bartender says, "What do you have?"*
*The guy says:*

A. "75 cents."
B. "A green tuxedo."
C. "A trip to the moon."
D. "I wanted to see time fly."

**Joke Number Three:**
*A duck walks into a bar and asks, "Got any grapes?"*
*The bartender, confused, tells the duck that no, his bar doesn't serve grapes. The duck thanks him and leaves.*
*The next day, the duck returns and says, "Got any grapes?"*
*Again, the bartender tells him that, no, the bar does not serve grapes, has never served grapes, and, furthermore, will never serve grapes. The duck, a little ruffled, thanks him and leaves.*
*The next day, the duck returns, but before he can say anything, the bartender begins to yell: "Listen, duck! This is a bar! We do not serve grapes! If you ever ask for grapes again, I will nail your stupid duck beak to the bar!"*
*The duck is silent for a moment, and then asks, "Got any nails?"*
*Confused, the bartender says no. "Good!" says the duck, then says:*

A. "That's a funny name for a mouse."
B. "Then whose monkey was it?"
C. "Got any grapes?"
D. "What did you order?"

**Joke Number Four:**
*As a butcher is shooing a dog from his shop, he sees $10 and a note in his mouth, which reads: "10 lamb chops, please."*

*Amazed, he takes the money, puts a bag of chops in the dog's mouth, and quickly closes the shop. He follows the dog and watches him wait for a green light, look both ways, and trot across the road to a bus stop. The dog checks the timetable and sits on the bench. When a bus arrives, he walks around to the front and looks at the number, then boards the bus. The butcher follows, dumbstruck.*

*As the bus travels out into the suburbs, the dog takes in the scenery. After a while he stands on his back paws to push the "stop" button, then the butcher follows him off.*

*The dog runs up to a house and drops his bag on the stoop. He goes back down the path, takes a big run, and throws himself—Whap—against the door. He does this again and again. No answer. So he jumps on a wall, walks around the garden, beats his head against a window, jumps off, and waits at the front door. A big guy opens it and starts cursing and pummeling the dog.*

*The butcher runs up screams at the guy: "What the hell are you doing? This dog's a genius!"*

*The owner responds:*

A. "Yesterday we were campaigning."
B. "Are you gonna eat that?"
C. "It's supposed to do that?"
D. "Genius, my eye. It's the second time this week he's forgotten his key!"

When listening to a joke, we all know there will be some unexpected twist and that everything preceding the punch line is a necessary part of the joke. We understand that the punch line can only use elements previously introduced. More accurately, the punch line must use elements previously introduced—otherwise, why introduce them? Long-form stories are no different from jokes in that they should be this precise.

## What it means to dramatize an idea

*Seeing is different than being told.*
—African proverb

I have often had conversations with people who will like a film or story because it deals with a certain subject, such as sexism or racism. Then, later, when I see the film, I will see that the subject has not been dealt with at all, only spoken about.

Look at this scene from *The Wizard of Oz*, where Dorothy meets the Scarecrow:

```
          THE WIZARD OF OZ
                 by
            Noel Langley
          Florence Ryerson
       and Edgar Allan Woolf
                1939


               DOROTHY
    ... you did say something, didn't
    you?


The Scarecrow shakes his head, then nods --
Dorothy looks at the Scarecrow as he nods his
head -- she speaks to him --


           DOROTHY (CONT'D)
    Are you doing that on purpose, or
    can't you make up your mind?


The Scarecrow explains -- shows his straw head
--
```

SCARECROW
That's the trouble. I can't make up
my mind. I haven't got a brain—only
straw.

DOROTHY
How can you talk if you haven't got
a brain?

SCARECROW
I don't know. But some people
without brains do an awful lot of
talking, don't they?

DOROTHY
Yes, I guess you're right.

*Dorothy steps over the fence and into the
cornfield.*

DOROTHY
Well, we haven't really met
properly, have we?

SCARECROW
Why, no.

*Dorothy curtsies.*

DOROTHY
How do you do?

SCARECROW
How do you do?

DOROTHY
Very well, thank you.

SCARECROW
Oh, I'm not feeling at all well. You
see, it's very tedious being stuck
up here all day long with a pole up
your back.

DOROTHY
Oh, dear—that must be terribly
uncomfortable. Can't you get down?

*Dorothy moves around to the back of the pole—*

SCARECROW
Down? No, you see, I'm—Well,—I'm—

DOROTHY
Oh, well, here—let me help you.

SCARECROW
Oh, that's very kind of you—very
kind.

*Dorothy examines the back of the Scarecrow as
she tries to unfasten him—*

DOROTHY
Well, oh, dear—I don't quite see how
I can—

SCARECROW
Of course, I'm not bright about

```
        things, but if you'll just.…
```

*Dorothy follows the Scarecrow's directions—*

```
                SCARECROW
        …bend the nail down in the back,
        maybe I'll slip off and…

                DOROTHY
        Oh.…
```

*Dorothy turns the nail and the Scarecrow falls to the ground.*

Here, the Scarecrow is introduced, and one of the first things he says is that he doesn't have a brain. But it is he who knows how best to get him off his pole, not Dorothy.

Here's another scene:

*Dorothy and Scarecrow come forward along Yellow Brick Road. Dorothy reacts as she sees an apple orchard. She goes up to one of the trees.*

```
                DOROTHY
        Oh—apples—Oh, look! Oh. Oh—
```

*Dorothy picks an apple off—reacts as the tree takes the apple back and slaps Dorothy's hand—*

```
                DOROTHY
        Ouch!
```

*First Tree opens its "mouth" and speaks to Dorothy.*

TREE
What do you think you're doing?

DOROTHY
We've been walking a long ways and I
was hungry and—Did you say.…

*The First Tree gestures as it speaks—*

FIRST TREE
She was hungry! Well, how would you
like to have someone come along and
pick something off of you?

DOROTHY
Oh, dear—I keep forgetting I'm not
in Kansas.

SCARECROW
Come along, Dorothy—you don't want
any of those apples. Hmm!

FIRST TREE
What do you mean—she doesn't want
any of those apples? Are you hinting
my apples aren't what they ought to
be?

SCARECROW
Oh, no! It's just that she doesn't
like little green.…

*The Tree reacts, makes a grab for the two—*

*the Scarecrow fights him off as Dorothy runs off,*
*the Scarecrow follows her.*

> TREE
>
> ...you...

> SCARECROW
>
> Go—Go!

> TREE
>
> ...Oh—Help—let me out. I'll give you
> little green worms.

> SCARECROW
>
> I'll show you how to get apples.

> TREE (o.s.)
>
> You can't...

*The First tree winds up, throws apples.*

> TREE
>
> ...do that to me! I'll...

*Scarecrow and Dorothy react as the apples*
*begin to hit them. Scarecrow falls back to the*
*road—*

> TREE
>
> ...show you!

*The Trees throw apples at Scarecrow and*
*Dorothy and Toto in the b.g.— The Scarecrow*
*rises, dodges about—*

<pre>
                    TREES
          You can't do that! You can't do
          that! Hey!
</pre>

*First Tree laughs as it throws apples.*

<pre>
                  SCARECROW
          Hooray!
</pre>

*Scarecrow picks up the apples.*

<pre>
                  SCARECROW
          Hooray! I guess that did it! Help
          yourself.
</pre>

There it is again. It is the Scarecrow who has the plan to get the apples, not Dorothy. Some of you may be thinking that this type of writing might be too obvious. But how many times have you seen *The Wizard of Oz* and never noticed that the Scarecrow comes up with all of the plans? It was invisible to you—invisible ink.

Here is a great little scene for the Lion, the Tin Man, and the Scarecrow. Remember, the Tin Man thinks he has no heart, and the Lion believes himself a coward.

*Tin Man, Lion and Scarecrow peer over the rocks.*

<pre>
                  SCARECROW
          That's the castle of the Wicked
          Witch! Dorothy's in that awful
          place!

                  TIN MAN
          Oh, I hate to think of her in there.
          We've got to get her out.
</pre>

*(cries)*

                    SCARECROW
          Don't cry now. We haven't got the
          oil-can with us and you've been
          squeaking enough as it is.

                      LION
          Who's them? Who's them?

*The Witch's Winkies marching about in the*
*Castle Courtyard.*
*The Lion tries to turn back, but others grab*
*him, push him forward—*

                    SCARECROW
          I've got a plan how to get in there.

                      LION
          Fine. He's got a plan.

                    SCARECROW
          And you're going to lead us.

                      LION
          Yeah. Me?

                    SCARECROW
          Yes, you.

                      LION
          I—I—I—I—gotta get her outta there?

                    SCARECROW
          That's right.

> LION
>
> All right, I'll go in there for
> Dorothy—Wicked Witch or no Wicked
> Witch—guards or no guards—
> I'll tear 'em apart.
> (growls)
> I may not come out alive, but I'm
> going in there. There's only
> one thing I want you fellows to do.
>
> SCARECROW AND TIN MAN
> What's that?
>
> LION
> Talk me out of it.

Again, we see that the Scarecrow has a plan, but we also see that the Tin Man has a heart because he tears up. And the Lion gets a chance to show his courage in the face of fear.

By the time we get to the end of *The Wizard of Oz*, we know (at least, subconsciously) that the foursome of the Lion, the Tin Man, the Scarecrow, and Dorothy already have what they've been seeking. We, as an audience, were able to figure it out, and with that comes satisfaction. This almost happens on a subconscious level.

This is what is meant by dramatization. It is showing rather than telling. We know that those things to which we have an emotional connection stick with us better than those for which we have none. Dramatization is a way to get your intellectual ideas across to your audience emotionally.

Do you think anyone watching *Terminator* for the first time thought to themselves: The theme of this film is that none of us knows how important our lives might be? Of course they didn't. What they thought was: RUN! Get the hell away from that thing! But believe me they got the message of the film, whether they can articulate it or not.

Don't be afraid to entertain—a spoon full of sugar helps the medicine go down.

*Jaws* is another example of a film that dramatizes, in a very entertaining way, its theme. The character of Chief Brody is terrified of the water. It is something we learn about him early on. At the end of the film, after he has killed the shark, his last line is, "You know, I used to hate the water." He learned that to face his fear was to conquer his fear. The shark was an external representation of Brody's internal fear. If you think that this is something I'm reading into the film, look at the evidence and ask yourself, why would killing a shark rid Brody of his fear of water? It doesn't make any logical sense, but it makes all the sense in the world, thematically.

The following is a story by Aesop.

**"Bundle of sticks"**
*Once there was a farmer whose many sons were always bickering and fighting with each other. One day the farmer called his sons together. He had with him a bundle of sticks tied together.*

*He commanded each son to take the bundle and break it in half. In turn they tried and failed. The farmer then untied the bundle, handed each son a single stick and told them to break the sticks now, which they did with ease.*

*"You see, my sons," said the farmer, "if you are of one mind and unite to assist each other, you will be unaffected by all the attacks of your enemies; but if you are divided among yourselves, you will be broken as easily as these sticks."*

Armature (moral): in unity there is strength.

Aesop lived nearly 3,000 years ago and his stories are still told. Not only are they told, they thrive. They are part of our everyday lives. Everyone knows what we mean when we say someone is a wolf in sheep's clothing. Or if we say someone has sour grapes. Or if we say of someone that he's crying wolf. All of these sayings are from Aesop's stories.

Why have stories told so long ago stuck around? It is because they had something to say about living as a human being in society, and people haven't changed much since 600 BC. And believe me, as long as there are people, we will have the same problems we have always had.

Aesop's armatures are often called morals, but whatever you call them, it all boils down to the fact that he had a point. Not only that, but he dramatized his point. The farmer in the "Bundle of sticks" story demonstrates his point to his sons rather than just telling them. This also demonstrates Aesop's point to the reader.

Just as with a joke, these short-form stories have no excess elements. Remember that this is true of any well-crafted story, regardless of length.

I included this story to *dramatize* the ideas of dramatization and armature.

## Theme beats logic

*Don't give me logic, give me emotion.*
—Billy Wilder's instructions to his writing partner, I.A.L. Diamond

Let's start to explore this idea of *theme* versus *logic* by looking at the film *Raising Arizona*. Nicolas Cage and Holly Hunter play a couple desperate to have a child. They eventually resort to stealing an infant from a couple with quintuplets.

When the hapless couple brings the baby home, they all pose for a family photo. This snapshot of the new family is followed immediately by a shot of a man's head popping out of a small mud hole. The man screams at the top of his lungs as rain pours down upon him. In the background, we can see a prison wall and searchlight. This man is escaping from prison. Is there any logic at all that says that a man escaping from prison should or would scream as he makes his escape? In fact, logic tells us just the opposite—a man escaping prison would be as quiet as can be. So why is it in the film? It's because theme beats logic, and the mud-soaked screaming man makes a thematic point.

Look where the scene falls in the film—right after the snapshot of the happy family. So what? Think about it: Everything in the scene about the screaming man is made to resemble a birth. The man pops up headfirst. They could have started with his fingers pushing up out of the mud. That would make more sense, logically, if the man is digging, but this scene is not about logic. The head, covered with dripping mud, emerges from a small hole. The man screams and screams and screams as he is "born" into the world. This is an ugly birth; there is something wrong with this birth. That's the thematic point that beats logic. Nothing good happens for the Nick Cage and Holly Hunter characters after they steal the child. In fact, the escaped convict, along with another, seeks refuge at the couple's home. Hunter and Cage have no choice but to house the criminals because the criminals know about the kidnapping and threaten to expose their secret. The couple has no end of trouble until, at the film's conclusion, they return the child to his rightful parents.

This is a situation in which the armature is not spoken but is evident in every decision made by the storytellers. The armature could be stated: It is wrong to deprive others of their happiness to gain your own. Or it could be stated: Nothing good can come from a bad deed.

You may have your own way of putting the film's armature into words; make sure you can back it up with solid, consistent evidence in the story's structure.

*Groundhog Day* and *Tootsie* have similar armatures: When the protagonists use their inside information to get the object of their desire into bed, it doesn't work. In both cases the plan should work, but doesn't, because it isn't right thematically.

In *Tootsie* the armature is set up very well. What you see in the first act is that Dustin Hoffman's character is a good actor, and what makes him a good actor is that he can't lie when he's acting. He has to be true to his character. In life he is a liar, particularly to women. Through living the life of a fictional woman who can be nothing but honest, Dustin's male alter ego learns to be honest with women.

One of my favorite examples of this is the story of *Groundhog Day*. I read somewhere that the studio wanted some kind of explanation as to why Bill Murray's character was reliving the same day over and over again. They wanted a gypsy curse or something along those lines. From what I understand, it was written and then cut because it didn't work. The reason, I think, is that it doesn't need a logical explanation. The audience understands why it is happening. It is what is supposed to happen thematically to teach Bill Murray a lesson. When he learns his lesson, the phenomenon stops and we all know why. We understand that "ever since that day" Bill Murray is a better man.

Remember that dramatizing the armature is a way of getting an intellectual idea across emotionally. If you learn to do this you'll move more people more often and more deeply.

Another favorite example of mine is in the 1968 version of *Planet of the Apes*. Here the armature is that "Man" is a violent and self-destructive creature. This point is hammered home again and again, topped off by the ending, which reveals that humans destroyed their own world.

Near the middle of the film, before the audience knows that the planet is, indeed, Earth, there is a courtroom scene. You see, the sentient apes of this world have discovered that Taylor (Charlton Heston) can speak. Humans on this world are mute. The courtroom scene takes place following this discovery.

Up till then, Taylor had been kept in a cage. There is no logical reason to have this scene in a courtroom. Why not have the scene at Taylor's cage? It all goes back to the armature that Man is a violent and self-destructive creature. This scene, *thematically*, is about putting humanity on trial. The storytellers even make a point of stripping Taylor of his clothes to make him appear more Adam-like. And it is no mistake that this scene *immediately* follows the discovery that Taylor possesses speech. Just *being* human, it seems, is a crime. It is a beautifully crafted scene that abandons logic for theme to support its armature.

## The use of clones

*Once upon a time there were three little pigs.... .*"

What I am calling *clones* have been called other names—*mirror characters* and *reflection characters*—but, whatever you call them, they are useful tools of the storyteller's craft.

A *clone* in story terms is a tool for showing, not telling. Clones are characters in your story that represent what could, should, or might happen to the protagonist if he or she takes a particular path. Two of the Three Little Pigs are clones. It is the failure of the first two pigs that allows us to measure the success of the last pig. This is a simple use of clones, and one of the most obvious to see.

But clones exist in more complicated stories as well. In J.R.R. Tolkien's *The Lord of the Rings*, the pitiful character of Gollum is used to show what might happen to the hero Frodo if he is seduced by the power of a magic ring. Just as in the story of the three pigs, we measure the success of one character by the failure of another.

In *Tootsie*, the woman who is the object of Dustin Hoffman's desire is dating a lying womanizer. In one scene, Dustin, as a woman, confronts the womanizer and tells him that he understands his womanizing ways better than he thinks. This is a way for Dustin to "see" and confront himself.

The television show *ER* uses clones to great effect. Often a character will have a problem that is then mirrored by a patient. If a doctor has a drinking problem, for instance, the next thing you know she is treating a drunk driver. With that, she, and we, see what might happen if the character doesn't change her ways.

Going back to *The Wizard of Oz*, all three of Dorothy's companions are clones. They, like she, are looking for something they already have. Having clones is a way of dramatizing ideas; again, a way of showing instead of telling. As I said earlier, the audience sees that Scarecrow has brains from the very first scene and it is reinforced throughout the story. Perhaps you remember the line, "Don't cry, you'll rust again," said to the

Tin Man. Hmm, turns out he does have a heart, after all.

John Steinbeck uses a cast of clones in his novel *Of Mice and Men*. The armature of that story is that people need companionship. It is dramatized as well as stated. If it has been awhile since you've read it, I suggest you reread it soon. It is amazingly well-crafted. He knows what he wants to say and says it over and over again in different ways. And he does give you an intellectual idea on an emotional level.

In the story, George and Lennie are two migrant workers who travel and work together. Lennie, being mentally challenged, is a lot of trouble for George, but George's need for companionship and his love for Lennie make the relationship worth the trouble. Other characters even comment on how strange it is for these two to travel together.

One of the first things to happen is that George discovers that Lennie is petting a dead mouse he is keeping in his pocket. Lennie is a huge man who has no sense of his own strength and had killed the mouse by accident. Lennie enjoys the companionship of small, soft animals, and is obsessed with one day having rabbits to take care of.

When the duo reaches the ranch where they are to work, one of the people they meet is the boss's wife. She often flirts with the ranch hands because her husband doesn't pay attention to her—she craves companionship.

On this ranch there is also an old man who has on old dog. The other hands in the bunkhouse think the dog is worthless. A man named Carlson suggests that the old man shoot the stinky old dog because it has, as he puts it, "'Got no teeth,' he said. 'He's all stiff with rheumatism. He ain't no good to you.'"

The scene goes on with Candy, the old man, protesting, but Carlson won't let go of his idea that the dog should be shot:

"Candy looked about unhappily. "No," he said softly. "No, I couldn't do that. I had 'im too long."
"He don't have no fun," Carlson insisted. "And he stinks to beat hell. Tell you what. I'll shoot him for you. Then it won't be you what does it."

Candy threw his legs off his bunk. He scratched the white stubble whiskers on his cheek nervously. "I'm so used to him," he said softly. "I had him from a pup."

"Well, you ain't bein' kind to him keepin' him alive," said Carlson. "Look, Slim's bitch got a litter right now. I bet Slim would give you one of them pups to raise up, wouldn't you, Slim?"

The skinner had been studying the old dog with his calm eyes. "Yeah," he said. "You can have a pup if you want to." He seemed to shake himself free for speech. "Carl's right, Candy. That dog ain't no good to himself. I wisht somebody'd shoot me if I get old an' a cripple."

Candy looked helplessly at him, for Slim's opinions were law. "Maybe it'd hurt him," he suggested. "I don't mind takin' care of him."

Carlson said: "The way I'd shoot him, he wouldn't feel nothing. I'd put the gun right there." He pointed with his toe. "Right back of the head. He wouldn't even quiver."

At last Carlson said: "If you want me to, I'll put the old devil out of his misery right now and get it over with. Ain't nothing left for him. Can't eat, can't see, can't even walk without hurtin'."

Candy said hopefully: "You ain't got no gun."

"The hell I ain't. Got a Luger. It won't hurt him none at all."

Candy said: "Maybe tomorra. Le's wait till tomorra."

"I don't see no reason for it," said Carlson. He went to his bunk, pulled his bag from underneath it, and took out a Luger pistol. "Let's get it over with," he said. "We can't sleep with him stinkin' around in here." He put the pistol in his hip pocket.

Candy looked a long time at Slim to try to find some reversal. And Slim gave him none. At last Candy said softly and hopelessly: "Awright—take 'im." He did not look down at the dog at all. He lay back on his bunk and crossed his arms behind his head and stared at the ceiling.

From his pocket Carlson took a little leather thong. He stooped over and tied it around the  dog's neck. All the men except Candy watched him.
"Come, boy. Come on, boy," he said gently. And he said apologetically to Candy: "He won't even feel it," Candy did not move nor answer him. He twitched the thong.
"Come on, boy." The old dog got slowly and stiffly to his feet and followed the gently-pulling leash."

Carlson takes the dog out to shoot him, and the old man lies on his back looking at the ceiling, and after an agonizingly long time, a shot is heard in the distance. With this, Candy rolls over in his bunk and faces the wall.

We see how much this stinky, old dog means to this man. The dog and the old man are clones of Lennie and George.

How do I know that I'm not reading all of this into the story? One way to know is the repetition of the armature. It is dramatized over and over again. The scene where they shoot the old man's dog is a well-written scene, but what makes it great is that it nails home the armature using emotion to do so.

Another way the point is nailed home is in the scene wherein George has gone to town with some of the other ranch hands, leaving Lennie alone. Lennie stumbles on Crooks, the black stable hand, in his shed next to the barn. Crooks is not allowed in the bunkhouse because he is black, and as a result is lonesome.  During their exchange Crooks says this to Lennie:

Crooks said gently: "Maybe you can see now. You got George. You know he's goin' to come back. S'pose you didn't have nobody. S'pose you couldn't go into the bunk-house and play rummy 'cause you was black. How'd you like that? S'pose you had to sit out here an' read books. Sure you could play horseshoes till it got dark, but then you got to read books. Books ain't no good. A guy needs somebody—to be near him." He whined: "A guy goes nuts if he ain't got nobody. Don't make

no difference who the guy is, long's he's with you. I tell
ya," he cried, "I tell ya a guy gets too lonely an' he gets sick."

As you can see, the armature is stated. I read or see stories all the time in
which characters say wise things and the audience nods knowingly, but
it means nothing if the structural elements of the story don't back it up.
Every decision one makes when constructing a story must contribute in
some way to the armature, or why is it there? Steinbeck makes good use
of clones in this story. And if you doubt for a minute the old man's dog
isn't a clone for Lennie, at one point Crooks speculates about Lennie
without George: "Want me ta tell ya what'll happen? They'll take ya to
the booby hatch. They'll tie ya up with a collar, like a dog."

Steinbeck was a master at the use of invisible ink. He understood
how secondary characters could help solidify his armature and dramatize
his point. One of the ironies of invisible ink is just how blatant one can
be when applying it. The audience will never see it unless they have been
trained to see the footprints in the grass.

Another master of invisible ink was storyteller Paddy Chayefsky.
He used clones with deft skill in his teleplay and movie *Marty*.

*Marty* was a television play written in the 1950s. It made such a
huge impact that the network was deluged with letters asking that it be
performed again. This was in the days of live television, and there were
no such things as reruns. Not only was it performed again, but also it was
made into a film that won the Best Picture Oscar™.

*Marty* is about an Italian-American man who can't seem to get
a date. He is considered ugly, and in his world he is also considered the
male equivalent of an old maid. He lives with his mother, who pesters
him to get married. These elements are the conflict in the piece. So, at
the fulcrum of the story, Marty finds a woman who likes him. Problem
solved. This is what both Marty and his mother have wanted. But here's
the thing about drama; lack of conflict kills it. So where does the conflict
come in now? Marty's mother has a clone, her sister. So what Chayefsky
does now is brilliant. After Marty meets his girlfriend, and it looks like
things are going well, Chayefsky cuts to this scene:

*Then the mother addresses herself to Aunt Catherine.*

                    MOTHER
        We gotta post card from my son,
        Nickie, and his bride this
        morning. They're in Florida inna big
        hotel. Everything is very nice.

                    AUNT
        That's nice.

                    MOTHER
        Catherine, I want you come live
        with me in my house with Marty and
        me. In my house, you have your
        own room. You don't have to sleep
        onna couch inna living room like
        here.

*The aunt looks slowly and directly at the mother.*

                 MOTHER (CONT'D)
        Catherine, your son is married. He
        got his own home. Leave him in
        peace. He wants to be alone with his
        wife. They don't want no old lady
        sitting inna balcony. Come and live
        with me. We will cook in the
        kitchen and talk like when we
        were girls. You are dear to me,
        and you are dear to Marty. We
        are pleased for you to come.

                    AUNT
Did they come to see you?

                    MOTHER
Yes.

                    AUNT
Did my son Thomas come with her?

                    MOTHER
Your son Thomas was there.

                    AUNT
Did he also say he wishes to cast
his mother from his house?

                    MOTHER
Catherine, don't make an opera outta
this. The three-a you anna baby live
in three skinny rooms. You are an
old goat, and she has an Italian
temper. She is a good girl, but
you drive her crazy. Leave them
alone. They have their own life.

*The old aunt turns her head slowly and looks
her sister square in the face. Then she rises
slowly from her chair.*

                    AUNT
[Coldly] Get outta here. This is my
son's house. This is where I live. I
am not to be cast out inna street
like a newspaper.

*The mother likewise rises. The two old women
face each other directly.*

MOTHER
Catherine, you are very dear to
me. We have cried many times
together. When my husband died,
I would have gone insane if it
were not for you. I ask you to come
to my house because I can make
you happy. Please come to my house.

*The two sisters regard each other. Then Aunt
Catherine sits again in her oaken chair, and
the mother returns to her seat. The hardened
muscles in the old aunt's face suddenly
slacken, and she turns to her sister.*

AUNT
Theresa, what shall become of me?

MOTHER
Catherine.

AUNT
It's gonna happen to you. Mark it
well. These terrible years. I'm
afraida look inna mirror. I'm
afraid I'm gonna see an old
lady with white hair, like the
old ladies inna park, little
bundles inna black shawl,
waiting for the coffin. I'm
fifty-six years old. What am I
to do with myself? I have
strength in my hands. I wanna cook.
I wanna clean. I wanna make dinner
for my children. I wanna be of use

                    AUNT (CONT)
         to somebody. Am I an old dog
         to lie in fronta the fire till my
         eyes close. These are terrible
         years, Theresa. Terrible years!

                    MOTHER
         Catherine, my sister…

*The old aunt stares, distraught, at the*
*mother.*

                    AUNT
         It's gonna happen to you! It's gonna
         happen to you! What will you do if
         Marty gets married! What will you
         cook?! What happen to alla children
         tumbling in alla rooms?! Where is
         the noise?! It is a curse to be a
         widow. A curse! What will you do if
         Marty gets married?! What will you
         do?!

*She stares at the mother—her deep, gaunt eyes*
*haggard and pained. The mother stares back for*
*a moment, then her own eyes close. The aunt*
*has hit home. The aunt sinks back onto her*
*chair, sitting stiffly, her arms on the thick*
*armrests. The mother sits hunched a little*
*forward, her hands nervously folded in her*
*lap.*

                    AUNT
         [Quietly] I will put my clothes
         inna bag and I will come to you
         tomorrow.

*The camera slowly dollies back from the two somber sisters.*

*[SLOW FADE-OUT.]*

This starts to worry Marty's mother and she changes her attitude about his getting married. It's very skillfully done and keeps the conflict, and therefore the interest, going.

Understand that not all stories use clones, but they are useful tools to put in your storyteller's toolbox. A storyteller should know why every character in their story exists. They should not be there just to "flesh out the world," as I often hear my students say.

In Alfred Hitchcock's *Rear Window*, Jimmy Stewart plays a man with a broken leg who doesn't want to marry his girlfriend, Grace Kelly.

Jimmy plays a photojournalist who lives a life of high adventure. In fact, he broke his leg while shooting a racecar accident. The reason he doesn't want to marry his fashion designer girlfriend is that he feels she doesn't have enough backbone. He feels they would be incompatible in a happily-ever-after situation.

Jimmy is confined to a wheelchair and so he passes the time by looking out his window and spying on his neighbors. The thing is, all of the neighbors are clones. They are all in various stages of romantic relationships. There is a honeymoon couple, an older childless couple, a sexy woman who has men fawning over her, a woman who can't get a date, and a couple that is always arguing—each one a distorted clone of Jimmy and Grace.

By the way, Jimmy changes his mind about Grace when he believes that one of his neighbors has murdered his wife and he sees just how much backbone she has as she throws herself into the adventure.

To the untrained eye, clone characters appear to be nothing more than secondary characters populating the story's world. But in the hands of a skillful storyteller, they are the invisible ink that helps illuminate the story's point.

| Chapter IV |

Ritual pain

Personal hell exercise

The crucifixion

From butterfly to caterpillar

Flip-flops

Characters who don't change

Killing the protagonist

## Ritual pain

*Everybody wants to go to heaven, but nobody wants to die.*
—Blues song lyric by D. Nix

So far I have mentioned character change, but without really discussing it. I will get to it in a few seconds.

A few years ago, when I was working on a spec screenplay that involved gangs, I visited a school with a lot of gang activity and asked the kids about how gangs worked. One of the things I found out was that in order to join a gang you had to be "jumped" in. What that means is that you let the other gang members beat the crap out of you for a proscribed amount of time, anywhere from two to five minutes. After that, you are a member of the gang.

This sounded so barbaric to me. I didn't understand why anyone would allow himself or herself to be abused in this way.

A couple of years after that, I was writing a comic book that had an Australian Aborigine as one of the main characters. While doing research, I read about one tribe that would knock one or two teeth out of adolescents as part of their initiation into adulthood.

I thought back on years earlier when a good friend of mine was rushing a fraternity. I never could have let myself be humiliated the way he allowed himself to be.

I began to see a pattern—groups of men or boys all have some kind of harsh initiation into their fold. It doesn't seem to be anything that has to be taught; it appears to be inherent behavior.

Later, I was talking with an African shaman who lived in my neighborhood and he began to talk about the manhood ceremony in his village. He talked about tribal peoples all over the world having similar ceremonies that involved what he called "ritual pain." Sometimes it is ritual scarification or tattooing. Sometimes it is a solo hunt for a beast. Other times it is to survive alone in the forest. In some cultures it involves a circumcision. Blood or the possibility of bloodletting is almost always part of the ritual. Like the street gangs say, "blood in, blood out." Meaning that you must undergo the pain to get into, or get out of, a gang.

In all cases, the purpose of this ritual seems to be about tearing the individual down and then transforming him from boyhood to manhood. At the end of the ritual he is considered a full-fledged member of the group with the rights, privileges, and responsibilities of an adult of said group.

I asked the shaman about women, and he thought that women don't usually have these kinds of ceremonies because they have a natural bloodletting that signifies their transformation from girls to women. Plus, they often have blood and/or pain when they lose their virginity. And we all know that there is pain in childbirth, and that certainly does change a woman. There is female circumcision, but it is imposed by men on women; therefore, it is not included here.

I started to think of this idea in story terms. The second act is a kind of ritual pain that changes your character. Usually your character has what has been called a fatal flaw. There is something they need to learn before they can be transformed into a better, more mature, person.

What is it that Elliot's brother says to him in E.T.? "Why don't you grow up and think how other people feel?"

We are all resistant to change. There is an old blues song that contains the lyric, "Everybody wants to go to heaven, but nobody wants to die."

There is more than likely something about yourself that you would like to change or that you should change but it is too difficult. I don't know why the world works this way, but the things we should do are always the most difficult. So we rarely run toward change. This is true of your characters as well.

In *Toy Story*, Buzz Lightyear won't believe that he is a toy and not a space ranger. Also in *Toy Story*, Woody has to learn to share the affection of his owner with Buzz. When you see the film again, you'll see that this transformation is not an easy one for them, but they are better "people" when they do change.

In *Toy Story 2*, Woody is in danger of being discarded and meets

Jesse, a clone, who tells him what his fate might be. It is painful for both of them, but they both realize that they have value.

Understanding story allowed Pixar to make one of the few sequels that measures up to the original. John Lasseter and the people at Pixar understand story as well as anyone. Study these films.

Look at *Jaws* again. Take a man afraid of the water, subject him to the ritual pain of doing battle with a shark, and that pain transforms him. Cures him.

James Cameron took what could have been a little B-movie and made *Terminator* into a surprise box office hit. He put Linda Hamilton's character, Sarah Connor, through the ritual pain of being hunted down and nearly killed. In the end she is transformed into a woman who knows that her life matters. She has also been hardened by the experience and seems less girlish. Grown up.

In *Terminator 2: Judgment Day*, Sarah Connor becomes the terminator. It is she who tries to kill a man for something he will do in the future. Through ritual pain she realizes that she has become the very thing she hates.

In *Aliens*, Cameron had Sigourney Weaver's character, Ripley, plagued by nightmares of the creature she had survived in the first film in the *Alien* series. Through the ritual pain of battling these creatures again, she purges herself of these nightmares and takes back her life.

Billy Wilder understood the power of character change so well that when the American Film Institute listed the top one hundred films of all time, four were his.

In *Sunset Boulevard*, Wilder had character Joe Gillis, an out-of-work Hollywood screenwriter, sell out for a little security and become the kept man of an older ex-movie star. He becomes her pet. In fact, when they first meet, the pet chimp of the has-been star has just died. It is no mistake that following this Joe Gillis moves into the woman's home. At one point in the film she dresses Joe in a tux—sometimes called a monkey suit. Through the ritual pain of being a kept man Joe Gillis learns that having a swimming pool isn't worth selling out his principles.

This idea of selling out shows up again and again in other Wilder films. In *The Apartment*, Jack Lemmon plays a man who, to climb the corporate ladder, lends his apartment to adulterous executives at the insurance company where he works. Sometimes this means not getting into his own apartment and having to sleep in the park. He, of course, learns to stand up for himself.

Also in *The Apartment*, Shirley MacLaine plays a woman who is having an affair with one of the aforementioned executives. This idea of selling out, or prostituting oneself, hits hard when the executive, not having time to buy a Christmas present for his mistress, hands Shirley a hundred dollar bill as a gift. It is through the ritual pain of being made to feel cheap that Shirley learns to respect herself enough to be with a man who will commit to her fully.

*The Apartment* has two characters who change, but they both learn essentially the same lesson. They are clones of one another.

Because change is never easy, and is resisted, it is your job as storyteller to apply as much pressure on your characters as possible. You must back them into a corner and force them to change. Make it as painful as you can. Bring them to the brink of physical or emotional death if you possibly can. Your protagonists will be measured by the size of their struggle, so don't pull any punches.

Those who believe in reincarnation believe that we die and are reborn until we learn whatever we were sent to learn in life. When we finally attain wisdom, we ascend to a higher plane of existence. We are rewarded.

You don't need to believe in reincarnation to see this idea played out. Many of us know people who repeat the same mistakes over and over in their lives. They might, for instance, keep dating people who disrespect them. Until they realize that they bring this on themselves, they will never be happy. They will never get their reward.

*Groundhog Day* is a great example of this concept in story form. Bill Murray is, in a sense, reborn every day. At one point he even tries to kill himself to get out of this cycle, but it doesn't work. It is only when he starts to focus on things outside of himself, and becomes a better person, that he is able to reap his reward. He then "ascends" and is able to move on to a higher level of existence.

A character always knows what he wants, but hardly ever what he needs. In the end, the character usually gets close to what he wants and chooses the need instead. For example, in *Casablanca*, Bogart gets the girl—the very thing he's wanted through the entire story. But he tells her to go with her husband. His need is to get over Ingrid Bergman. When he is holding tightly to his want he is a bitter, selfish man. He even says, "I stick my neck out for no one." In the end, he risks his neck to assure that the woman he loves can leave with her husband. We know he is a better person. He has grown. He has ascended.

In *The Apartment*, Jack Lemmon gets the promotion he's been after from the beginning of the story. But he is done compromising his self-respect, and turns down the job. He has ascended. This act helps him get his real reward, the woman he loves.

In *E.T.*, Elliot wants his friend to stay with him, but helps him get home. He puts the needs of his friend ahead of his own desires. It is painful for him, but it is the right thing to do. Elliot ascends to a better place through suffering ritual pain.

Most viewers of *E.T.* are unaware that they are watching the transformation of a character from a selfish child to a caring human being, but they do feel it.

Ritual pain means painfully killing off one aspect of a character's personality to make room for something new.

Character transformation and growth are some of the most powerful forms of invisible ink, and you would do well to include them in your work.

# Personal hell exercise

This exercise is to show you how to come up with the type of ritual pain appropriate for your character.

In Greek mythology, Persephone, daughter of Zeus and Demeter, was abducted by Hades and taken to the underworld, the realm of the dead.

I was just reading this story and realized that all characters of change take a journey to the underworld. Characters must confront the very thing they would least like to, and confronting this thing is a kind of hell. More precisely, it is their own personal hell. But through this confrontation, they are transformed.

Let's revisit our friend, King Midas. If all the king wants is gold, then as a storyteller creating that story, one would have to find a way to put Midas in hell, to take him to the underworld. The storyteller granted the King his wish that everything Midas touched turned to gold. It wasn't long before King Midas realized that this blessing was a curse when he changed his beloved daughter into gold. Midas learns that some things are more precious than gold. A trip to one's personal hell changes one.

In the movie *Jaws*, a man is deathly afraid of the water, so where do you suppose his personal hell is? In the middle of the ocean where a vicious shark swims about, that's where.

"Snakes. Why did it have to be snakes?" says Indiana Jones in *Raiders of the Lost Ark*, when he finds he must descend into a pit of the slithering reptiles. But we know why it had to be snakes—it's because as we find out early on in the film, Indiana Jones hates snakes. To get the prize he seeks, he must take a trip to the underworld, to his own personal hell.

In the classic film *It's a Wonderful Life*, George Bailey wishes he had never been born. In his personal hell, he is granted the chance to see what the world would be like without him, and it's not a pretty place.

In Alfred Hitchcock's *Shadow of a Doubt*, a young woman wishes she had more excitement in her life. She gets more excitement when her favorite uncle comes to town and turns out to be a murderer.

In *The Wizard of Oz*, Dorothy wants to run away from home, so a twister takes her far away. And, of course, all she wants is to get back home, because she is in her personal hell.

In *Finding Nemo*, the father desperately tries to keep his son safe by never letting him out of his sight, and keeping him close to home. What happens? His son is taken away into the ocean. This is the father's personal hell.

"Of all the gin joints in all the world she had to walk into mine," goes Bogart's famous line from the film *Casablanca*. He says this because the woman he was in love with, and wants to forget, has just come into his world. This is his personal hell.

This is one of the simplest ways to apply invisible ink to your work, but it will yield powerful results. It is a simple way to find out what your story needs to be about. Find that thing that your character would rather die than do and make them do it.

Here is an exercise. Write down the personal hell for the characters provided below. There is no right answer, just make sure the characters go to that place, or do that thing they would least like.

**Example:** A rich man wants nothing more than to acquire more money.

Personal hell: He finds himself penniless.

**Example:** A girl wants to run away from home.

Personal hell: She gets her wish and wants nothing more than to get home.

**Your turn:**

**Character:** A vain woman cares about nothing but her looks.

Personal hell: _____

**Character:** A woman hates people and wants to spend all of her time alone.

Personal hell: _____

Character: A man wants fame more than anything.

Personal hell: _____

Character: A man won't let go of the past and move on with his life.

Personal hell: _____

**Character:** A man has spent his life as an assassin.

Personal hell: _____

**Character:** A woman is so into cleanliness that she won't even let people into her home.

Personal hell: _____

**Character:** A man is a lying womanizer.

Personal hell: _____

**Character:** A woman dates only very wealthy men.

Personal hell: _____

**Character:** A man wants to spend his life traveling the world.

Personal hell: _____

**Character:** An honest cop.

Personal hell: _____

**Character:** An inventor believes his technology to be infallible.

Personal hell: _____

**Character:** A spoiled child.

Personal hell: _____

## The crucifixion

*What we do for ourselves dies with us. What we do for others is immortal.*
—Albert Pine

Sacrifice is an important part of what makes a protagonist a hero. Few of us have much respect for someone who has had things too easy. We admire struggle and sacrifice.

I remember hearing a story about a man in a Nazi death camp who volunteered to take the place of another man who was slated to be killed. The first man had a family and begged the Nazis to spare him. The second man had no family and so sacrificed himself for the first man and his family. Few of us would do such a thing, though we all wish we would. That's what makes a hero—someone who puts the needs of others before his own.

George Bailey, in *It's a Wonderful Life*, spends his entire life sacrificing for others. We see him as a heroic figure because of that self-sacrifice.

You might think that this is visible ink, but readers and audiences are unaware of its use when it is applied skillfully.

Look at the story of the crucifixion. Jesus is suffering on the cross. It's important that this aspect of the story be relayed to us. Remember that this is the Son of God, here; he can work miracles. So we might very well wonder if he suffered at all up there. His crown of thorns, his having to carry his own cross, his stab wound, are all necessary details of the narrative.

Jesus even says, "Father, why have you forsaken me?" It is important for us to know that he was not, through some miracle, spared the pain of the crucifixion. The story's power lies in the idea that he suffered just as you or I would have. Like all great heroes, Jesus' suffering is for others.

And then, of course, what happens to Jesus? He rises from the grave. He ascends to heaven. He is rewarded for his pain.

According to Norse mythology, the king of the gods, Odin, gave up one of his eyes and was speared to a tree for nine days in order to gain wisdom. Attaining wisdom is never easy.

In *The Adventures of Huckleberry Finn*, Huck isn't sure if he should turn in Jim, the runaway slave. His world tells him it is a sin not to do so. But Huck has come to know and care for Jim and to see him as a human being.

At the end of the book, Huck decides that he'd rather sin than turn in his friend.

"I'll go to hell then," he says. He believes he will be punished forever for helping his friend. This is a pretty big sacrifice.

We even respect small sacrifices. One of my best friends is always willing to admit when he's wrong. He owns up to it quicker than anyone I've ever met. Not just with small things, either. How many of us are so willing to admit our mistakes and shortcomings? I'm not saying that my friend is a hero, but there is a certain amount of courage involved in being the type of person that he is. He leaves himself vulnerable emotionally, and emotional pain can be just as damaging as physical pain, sometimes more.

In *Terminator 2*, the robot from the future sacrifices himself for the good of humanity. This once-murderous machine is now a hero.

All characters of change have, at least, an emotional death that allows them to be resurrected anew.

Apply enough pressure and heat to change a lump of coal into a diamond.

## From butterfly to caterpillar

*If once you start down the dark path, forever will it dominate your destiny.*
—Yoda, *The Empire Strikes Back*

Characters don't always change for the better. Some stories are about how people are corrupted—how angels fall.

In *The Godfather*, Michael Corleone starts off as a virtuous man—a war hero, no less. When he tells his fiancée, Kay, about his family's criminal behavior, he tells her, "That's my family, Kay, not me." He is above all of this.

What is the ritual pain that begins his change? His father is shot. Michael may not approve of his family's business, but he does care for them.

His change is slow at first. First, he protects his father while the men who shot him try to finish him off. As an audience we can understand that. Who wouldn't protect someone they love from killers?

Then Michael decides he wants to kill the men who shot his father. When he does kill them, it is not justice, it is revenge. Michael's father was not killed, only wounded.

That might not make much difference in some story realities, but it does in this one. We know that because in the opening scene Michael's own father tells us so. He defines the difference between justice and revenge when a man comes to him asking him to kill the two men who nearly raped his daughter.

> BONASERA
> What do you want of me? I'll give you anything you want, but do what I ask!

> DON CORLEONE
> And what is that Bonasera?

```
          BONASERA
(whispers into the DON's ear.)


        DON CORLEONE
No. You ask for too much.


          BONASERA
I ask for justice.


        DON CORLEONE
The Court gave you justice.


          BONASERA
An eye for an eye!


        DON CORLEONE
But your daughter is still alive.
```

So as an audience we know when Michael has crossed onto the "dark path." And we have seen how someone can be seduced into this world. The angel has fallen.

Because the scene with Don Corleone and Bonasera is the first scene in the film, it becomes invisible ink. The audience has no idea that this scene will help them understand the rest of the film. Like all forms of invisible ink, it works on a subconscious level.

## Flip-flops

When I say flip-flops I don't mean shoes. Flip-flops is the name that I give characters who are opposites, but exchange character traits.

Oscar and Felix of Neil Simon's play *The Odd Couple* are probably the most famous flip-flops. One is clean and prissy while the other is sloppy and gruff. Their marriages have broken up and they are thrown together as roommates. They are extreme opposites, which offers the best opportunity for conflict and, therefore, comedy. Their ritual pain is having to live with one another.

By the end of the story we have seen why both of their marriages failed. This pairing is a replay, or a clone, of each of their marriages. But it has also changed both characters. Both are a little more aware of their respective faults. They could each stand to be a little bit like the other.

In fact, the last messy thing Oscar does is tell his poker guests to watch their cigarette ashes. He says, " This is my house, not a pigsty." This is a huge change from the Oscar at the opening of the play.

Another classic example is *The African Queen*. In that film, Humphrey Bogart plays a crusty, hard-drinking boat captain, while Katharine Hepburn plays his flip-flop. She is a stuffy religious matron who detests vulgar vices such as demon rum. These two share little in common except the small boat they are trapped on together.

Through the ritual pain of having to make their way down a treacherous river together, they both become fuller people. Each has something the other is lacking, and by exchanging traits they become whole.

Sometimes only one of the characters needs to change and the other is the catalyst for that change, such as in *Beauty and the Beast*. When the Beast changes enough on the inside to earn the love of a woman, he changes on the outside from a beast to a handsome man. The change is only an external manifestation of what is going on internally.

*Shrek* turns this idea on its green funnel-shaped ear, but it is still the same story. Shrek is completely comfortable with who he is; it is the Princess who must change.

## Characters who don't change

Do characters always need to change? No, they don't. But you always have to remember what your armature is and why you are telling the story. Let that make the decision for you. What is the best way to dramatize your point?

This is not exactly the story of an individual who doesn't change, but it illustrates my point quite well, I think: When I was a kid, I learned a lot about story structure by watching old reruns of Rod Serling's *The Twilight Zone*. There is one episode called "It's a Good Life." In it, an evil five-year-old boy, who has the power to read minds and do just about anything else, has the small farm town of Peaksville, Ohio, held captive. For all intents and purposes, the rest of the world has ceased to exist.

The few people left in the town walk on eggshells so as not to suffer the boy's wrath. They are all miserable, but they try only to say good things and think good thoughts. The boy might hear their bad thoughts, were they to have them, and kill them in some cruel fashion, like setting them on fire, or worse. He even kills a couple of "clone" animals so that we, the audience, get an idea of his power. Even the boy's parents live in fear.

One night, there is a birthday gathering for one of the townsfolk at the house of the boy. The guest of honor receives a few gifts from what can be scrounged up by his friends. The town is running low on food and other provisions and luxuries, but the boy neglects to replenish them.

The boy likes music but hates singing, and one of the gifts received by the man having the birthday is a record of his favorite singer. He wants desperately to play it, but the others warn against it. Upset, he starts in on another gift, a bottle of rye whiskey. He gets drunk and starts to complain out loud for all to hear.

The other adults are in a panic—they try to distract the boy and calm the man down, but he's having none of it. Surprisingly, the boy ignores the man's drunken rant. But the man just gets louder and more obnoxious. (We, the audience, know something bad will happen, but the storytellers drag this scene out an agonizingly long time. They understood that promising conflict was a powerful form of invisible ink.)

In a final act of defiance, the man tries to get his fellow captives to join him in a rousing chorus of "Happy Birthday." The boy loses his patience and glowers at the man.

The man's song is directed right at the boy and it becomes clear that this is a kind of suicide. When it is clear that all the boy's attention is on him, the man tries to get someone to come up behind the boy and kill him. He begs them to take the risk. Sure, they might be killed, but if they were to succeed all of this misery would be over.

The people do nothing. The boy kills the man in a rather grotesque manner.

With that, the boy's father notices that his son is making it snow outside. He loses his temper because the snow will ruin the crops. He begins to yell at the boy, but catches himself and tells the boy that it's good that he's making it snow.

The end.

This story is more about a situation that remains the same rather than one character, but you get the idea.

What is the armature of this story, do you think? It tells us that no one has any power over us that we don't give to them. It is better to challenge oppression and die than to live under its thumb. Gandhi brought down the British Empire by simply not acknowledging their power in his country. That's it.

The drunken man in this piece becomes the hero. He made a sacrifice hoping that it would help those left behind. The others are seen as cowards.

So how did the storytellers get away with not changing things? For one thing, it was the best way to make the point. And for another, we saw where things could have changed but didn't. If only they had stood up to the boy—to their oppressor. The fork in the road that let the audience know what could happen is a kind of invisible ink.

The ending with the snow is important because we see that things are going to continue to be the same—"and ever since that day."

**Killing the protagonist**

*A man who has nothing he would die for isn't fit to live.*
—Martin Luther King, Jr.

If you can have your protagonist make the ultimate sacrifice, that's great. But make sure they finish their story first. What I mean is, if you kill the character in the middle of their journey, it isn't satisfying.

One of the most famous protagonist deaths is that of Janet Leigh in *Psycho*. I've heard much talk about how shocking that death was to people at the time, and how it was so groundbreaking. I'm sure it was, but Mr. Hitchcock and screenwriter Joseph Stefano still played by the rules. Janet Leigh's character was done with her story.

In *Psycho*, Janet Leigh plays a woman, Marion Crane, who steals money from her boss. She skips town and winds up at the Bates Motel where she meets Norman. Norman makes them sandwiches that they eat in a back room of the motel. There they have this conversation about Norman's situation with his "mother."

> MARION
> Why don't you go away?

> NORMAN
> To a private island, like you?

> MARION
> No, not like me.

> NORMAN
> I couldn't do that. Who'd look after
> her? She'd be alone up there. The
> fire would go out. It'd be cold
> and damp like a grave. If you
> love someone, you don't do that

to them even if you hate them. You
understand that I don't hate her—I
hate what she's become. I hate the
illness.

MARION

Wouldn't it be better—if you put
her—someplace—?

*Norman's demeanor darkens. He leans forward.*

NORMAN

You mean an institution? A madhouse!
People always call a madhouse
'someplace,' don't they. 'Put her
in—someplace.'

MARION

I-I'm sorry. I didn't mean it to
sound uncaring.

NORMAN

What do you know about caring. Have
you ever seen the inside of one
of those places? The laughing
and the tears—and the cruel
eyes studying you. My mother there!
But she's harmless! Wh—she's as
harmless as one of those stuffed
birds!

MARION

I am sorry. I only felt—it seems
she's hurting you. I meant well.

*Marion is more than a little spooked by his personality transformation.*

                NORMAN:

People always mean well! They
cluck their thick tongues and
shake their heads and suggest,
oh so very delicately—! (He sits
back. The storm is over. Gently:)
Of course, I've suggested it
myself. But I hate to even think
about it. She needs me. It—it's
not as if she were a—a maniac—a
raving thing. She just goes a
little mad sometimes. We all go a
little mad sometimes. Haven't you?

                MARION
          (*her concern relaxed*)
Yes. Sometimes just one time can be
enough. Thank you.

                NORMAN
'Thank you, Norman.'

                MARION
Norman.

                NORMAN
Oh, you're not—you're not going back
to your room already?

                MARION
I'm very tired. And I have a long

```
                    MARION (CONT'D)
          drive tomorrow—all the way back to
          Phoenix.


                    NORMAN
          Really?


                    MARION
          I stepped into a private trap back
          there and I'd like to go back and
          try to pull myself out of it before
          it's too late for me to.
```

*She stands to go.*


At the end of this scene, Marion has decided to give back the money. She is better now, so although we may be shocked that she is killed, we do not feel cheated.

Thelma, in *Thelma and Louise*, takes on some of the traits of Louise and becomes a stronger person. Her thematic journey is over and it is okay if she dies. We may be sad, but again, we do not feel cheated.

Billy Wilder killed a few protagonists in his day. In *Sunset Boulevard*, Joe Gillis is killed off at the end, after he has made his transformation for the better. Few people have written a script as well-constructed as Sunset Boulevard—with, of course, the exception of Wilder himself.

In *Ace in the Hole* (aka *The Big Carnival*), Kirk Douglas plays a down-and-out reporter who finds a way to keep a man trapped in a cave in order to milk the story for as long as he can. He wants to be back on top again. He wants a Pulitzer Prize.

The reporter convinces others to go along with his plan, all for their own selfish reasons, including the engineer in charge of digging the man out. Eventually the man takes ill and it becomes clear he will die. This starts to change the reporter, he starts to feel guilty about what he's done, and now there is no time to get the man out.

The reporter ends up being stabbed in the belly (you'll have to see the film to see how). Instead of tending to his own wounds, he rushes to a church to get a priest to give the trapped man his last rites before he dies. He also confesses to what he's done, before he himself dies.

By not tending to his own wounds he sacrificed his own life so that the other man could have his last rites. We know that the reporter was a better human being when he died than he was at the story's start.

What about *Butch Cassidy and the Sundance Kid*? After all, they don't get better before they die. That is true, they don't. But there is that fork in the road where they could go straight. They even try it, but it's not for them.

Before the escape to Bolivia, they are pursued by a super-posse that is almost supernatural. This could easily be seen as Death pursuing them. If they don't change their ways eventually, Death will catch up to them. They refuse to change with the times and choose to go out in a blaze of glory. As with the episode of *The Twilight Zone* mentioned before, it is important to see that there was another road that was not taken.

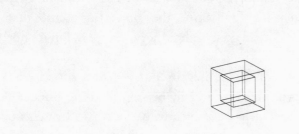

| Chapter V |

Tell the truth

The masculine and the feminine

Drama in real life

The myth of genre

Climax

God from the machine

Supporting plots (sub-plots)

Slave, not master

## Tell the truth

*We must never forget that art is not a form of propaganda; it is a form of truth.*
—John F. Kennedy

I f you take nothing else away from this book, remember always to tell the truth, the whole truth, and nothing but the truth. If you do this always, you will be a master storyteller. This is much harder than it sounds.

What does it mean to tell the truth when writing fiction? For one thing, it is not about facts. Storytellers are not concerned with facts, just truth. Sometimes facts can even get in the way of the truth.

When you are watching a horror movie and you know that the girl in the tank top and panties shouldn't go into the basement alone, and you know she has other options, but she goes into the basement anyway—that's a lie. It only happened because the storytellers wanted it to happen, but not because it was a logical thing a reasonable person would do.

On the other hand, if the girl does everything you would do, and is even a little smarter but the monster gets her anyway—now that's scary.

You want to see truth in fiction? Watch Jimmy Stewart's breakdown in *It's a Wonderful Life*, just before he decides to kill himself. It's about as real and truthful as anything you'll ever see on film. Capra is known for being lighthearted, but when he got dark, he always told the truth. If you want to affect people deeply, tell the truth.

Remember in *Big* when Tom Hanks has gotten his wish and has become an adult? Remember his first night away from home in the sleazy hotel? He cried. This is a comedy, right? But when Hanks cries in that scene, nobody's laughing. In fact, it's painful to watch. The filmmakers played the truth of the scene.

The Donner Party was a group of pioneers in the 1840s who got snowed in in the mountains and resorted to cannibalism to survive. This is not light subject matter. Charlie Chaplin read about this incident and thought, Now that's funny!

The Donner Party inspired one of Chaplin's most famous scenes from one of his most famous films. In *The Gold Rush*, he plays a man trapped in a small cabin in the snow along with another unfortunate soul. They are starving. And even though some humor comes out of the situation, you never forget that these men are truly hungry.

With nothing left to eat, Chaplin cooks, and serves up, his leather shoe. Chaplin treats the shoe like a spaghetti dinner. He eats it like he's eating a fine meal. He makes the tragic funny. I'm not the first to say it, but the truth is funny.

*Raiders of the Lost Ark* has a great example of truth in it. There is a scene in which a scary opponent who dazzles us with dangerous-looking swordsmanship, confronts Indiana Jones. I remember sitting in the theater on the edge of my seat, expecting an exciting action sequence. But instead, Indy calmly pulls out his gun and shoots the man dead. Anyone who saw that in the theater remembers the uproar of laughter that followed. Why was it so funny? It was the truth. It was the most logical thing for Indiana to do.

On the old *Batman* television show, the villains would always construct some Rube Goldberg-like contraption to kill Batman. Even little kids wondered why no one ever pulled out a gun and shot him. It was a lie and we all knew it.

Lying is visible ink. It is easy for the audience to see and therefore doesn't work.

*Roseanne* changed the face of television because she refused to lie on her show. She played the first "real" mother on television.

The film *Election* has some amazingly honest work in it. In one scene, a girl gives a speech at a school assembly, a speech that is so honest as to how most of us felt about high school that it seems like she's reading from your own diary.

In that same film Matthew Broderick has a scene where he is preparing for a sexual escapade by washing his genitals in the tub. Few of us would admit to doing such a thing in public, but a theater full of people will howl with the laughter of recognition. The film was raw with the honesty of human behavior.

Most writers are afraid to put something so personal down on paper. We think that it is a window into our own personal lives, and we don't want to be judged by it. But here's the big secret—we are all the same. The more you dip into your own behavior, good or bad—the more others will see themselves, and you will fade into the background.

Several decades after World War II, color movie footage of Hitler was discovered. Some people thought it shouldn't be shown because it humanized a monster. But that is what makes Hitler a monster—he was a human being, not some creature from outer space. It makes a much stronger point not to shy away from that fact. It means if we are not careful, we may produce another monster.

It is the same with a hero. If you can show that a hero had fears, doubts, and human foibles but did a heroic thing anyway, it makes him all the more heroic.

The worst of us has good in him and the best of us has some bad. That is a truth that many of us want to deny, but as storytellers it is the truth we must illuminate.

The truth will always be sadder, happier, funnier, scarier, and more profound than the best lie. More importantly, the audience never "sees" it, but does feel it.

# The masculine and the feminine

*'The King died and then the Queen died' is a story. 'The King died and then the Queen died of grief' is a plot.*
—E. M. Forster

The quote above is often used to define the difference between plot and story, but I'm not going to use it for that. I'm going to use it for what I call the "masculine" and "feminine" elements of story.

First, a little background. I was watching Shirley MacLaine on *Inside the Actor's Studio* and she was asked what time of day she likes to write. She answered that if she was writing about the present, she liked to write by the masculine energy of the sun, and if she was writing about the distant past, she liked to write by the feminine energy of the moon.

The concept of seeing the moon as feminine and the sun as masculine seemed to make sense to me, in an ancient sort of way. And for some reason it stuck with me and I began to look at the two attributes in terms of story. Then I had, what was for me, an epiphany: there are masculine and feminine elements of story.

When I put this hypothesis to the test, and applied it to classic stories that have worked over time, it held up. When I then applied it to my own work, it elevated the level of my stories. When I told friends and students, they also found that it helped them.

I define masculine elements as external, while feminine elements are internal. Without equal, or close to equal, parts, your story is unbalanced.

Consider the way most of us think of comic book stories—a square-jawed hero who is all good and never questions himself. Its concept of good and evil, right and wrong, is cartoonish. There is no gray, only black and white. Everything is on the surface. It is external. This is masculine.

Now consider the typical soap opera. It is all about evoking emotion. The outrageousness of the situation doesn't matter as long as it leads to a strong emotional response. It is all about what characters are experiencing inside. This is feminine.

There are action films, full of excitement, in which lots of things blow up and tons of people are killed, which men just love and which bore most women stiff because they are devoid of emotion.

Conversely, there are stories that bore men because they seem so slow and plodding—films that deal with the emotional lives of people but seem to have no story or forward movement.

Allow me to generalize here: Who buys pornography and who buys romance novels? One is all external and devoid of emotion and the other is largely internal and all about emotion. Both are unreal fantasy worlds. In movie-world vernacular they are "boy movies" and "chick flicks."

Why is it that all of these forms—mindless action films, soap operas, comic books, pornography, and romance novels—are considered "trash" by most of us? Even those of us who indulge in them regard them as guilty pleasures. It is because they are unbalanced.

Understand that I'm not saying that one, feminine or masculine, is better or worse than the other. On the contrary, I am saying that one without the other is a lie. Again, our job as storytellers is to tell the truth. Your stories will have much more resonance if you do.

It is a lie to have a man mow down fifty people in a story, with no consequences. There are consequences when people are murdered. There is an impact on the families of those killed, on the communities where they live, and more than likely on the killer.

Even in morally ambiguous worlds, such as those of *Goodfellas* or *The Godfather*, there are consequences for murder. The murderer becomes a target.

"He who lives by the sword shall die by the sword." This is not simple moralizing or preaching. Even in headhunting societies, the reason that they shrink heads and sew up the mouths and eyes of their victims is to keep the vengeful spirit within contained. Even in a culture where murder is condoned, they sense consequences.

This is why stories that ignore these consequences are considered unreal cartoons.

They are hollow, with no real point.

I can't tell you how many screenplays by men I've read that have no emotional or thematic life whatsoever. They are all about plot. Lots of things happen, but without any real purpose.

I have also read many scripts by women where plot and action take a backseat to emotional matters.

This is where I'm sure many of you want to kill the messenger, but I have seen it over and over again. I'm sure other writing teachers will tell you the same thing. Please don't have a knee-jerk reaction to this concept. You may fall at either end of the spectrum, regardless of your sex. Remember, I am generalizing. But I have noticed it to be generally true. And it is my job to tell the truth.

More specifically, how do I define masculine and feminine traits?

Masculine traits are anything that moves the story forward externally. For example, Character A, a policeman, finds out that the murderer in the case he's investigating is another cop. That is a masculine element.

The murdering cop is Character A's best friend and once risked his life to save Character A. This is a female element. It is the balance of these two elements that creates dramatic tension and keeps an audience interested. It keeps their brains working: What is Character A going to do? It creates depth.

Even in E. M. Forster's example of story and plot he uses the King to express the male and the Queen to express the female. It appears that Forster too recognized this on some level.

Remember The Donner Party? They were the group of snowbound pioneers who were forced to eat their dead to survive, and that Chaplin had read about.

Saying that they ate their dead is a purely factual statement devoid of emotion.

The following is the diary entry of one of the party members:

> [According to Mary Graves, as reported by Elizabeth Farnham
> in *California In-Doors and Out*, published in 1856]
> The morning came, and still the flood fell. They roused
> themselves to move on a little, if it were possible, despite the
> storm; but they had lost their course, and the sun no longer
> befriended them. It was proposed to return to the cabins,
> following their own tracks, but the Indians would not consent,
> and Miss G. resolutely determined to follow them. There was
> nothing possible, there, but starvation. The fate before them
> could not be worse, and might be better. Miss G.'s resolution
> encouraged her companions. They went on all day without
> a morsel of food, the rain pouring continuously. At night
> it ceased. Some were confused in their perceptions, some
> delirious, some raving. Those who were strong enough to realize
> their condition, might well now despair. The women bore up
> better than the men. One of them had a cape or mantle stuffed
> with raw cotton, and upon a minute examination of it, she
> found, between the shoulders, about an inch square of the inner
> surface dry. The lining was cut, and enough taken out to catch
> the spark from the flint. They lost or left their axe, but were able
> to make a fire, after much difficulty, of a few gathered boughs.
> They sat down around it. There was nothing else to be done

Here's a third-part account published a few years later:

> [According to Mary Thornton in Oregon and California in
> 1848, published in 1864] The snow beginning to fall, they
> all sat down to hold a council for the purpose of determining
> whether to proceed. All the men but Mr. Eddy refused to go
> forward. The women and Mr. Eddy declared they would go
> through or perish. Many reasons were urged for returning, and
> among others the fact that they had not tasted food for two

days, and this after having been on an allowance of one ounce per meal. It was said that they must all perish for want of food. At length, Patrick Dolan proposed that they should cast lots to see who should die, to furnish food for those who survived.

See how including emotional details gives the incident so much more impact than just the external facts? It creates dramatic tension.

As I said before, one cannot draw a line and say that all male writers write this way and that all female writers write the other way. But since discovering this concept, I have made certain observations about what kinds of people cross the line.

Actors, dancers, visual artists, poets, playwrights, English and literature majors tend to fall more on the feminine side of things, regardless of their gender. These people tend to put a lot more emphasis on character, the beauty of words, scenery, mood, and theme. Plot is seen by many of these people as cheap.

Films and books that are more feminine usually do better among critics and intellectuals, but seldom bring in a wide audience. They are often called "character- driven." Critics will often believe that these stories are too "smart" for the masses. Too cerebral, they might say.

Video gamers, mainstream comic book readers or creators, and action film fans tend to fall in the masculine category. Again, this is regardless of gender.

Stories with an emphasis on the visceral tend to do better with audiences. This is why the summer film releases are big budget special effects extravaganzas. People have fun going to films like this, but don't expect to get caught up emotionally in the content—and they seldom are. Other than an "Ooh," an "Ahh," or a "Wow—that blowed up real good!"

I like to see a good explosion as much as the next guy, but I want to care about what or who is blowing up. In *Jaws*, the shark is blown up at the end, but it matters storywise, and its one explosion has more impact than ten explosions in other films. Storytellers often feel that you either have one kind of story or another, but it is the balance that gets you the best of both worlds—a fun story to watch or read that has resonance for the audience. If you aren't trying to speak to an audience, why bother to write it down?

This is not about writing down to members of your audience. This is about writing for them. It is not their job to understand you; it is your job to communicate with them. And if you use drama to find an emotional way to give them an intellectual idea, they will "get it." They may not be able to articulate the idea, but they will understand it on a level beyond articulation.

Actors often talk about giving characters vulnerability. I think this is just another way of talking about the internal, emotional life of a character. Without this quality, characters are caricatures, not fully realized human beings.

The character of Quint in *Jaws* is a virtual cartoon of a salty old sailor until he delivers a speech about a terrifying experience he had with a shark attack. At that moment, a character who had shown nothing but a crusty exterior opens up and becomes human. This combination of masculine and feminine traits tells the truth about being a human being. One without the other is a lie and we know it. We feel it.

You have more than likely heard conflict broken down this way:

Man against Man;

Man against Nature;

Man against Himself.

I have seen *Jaws* described as Man against Nature. Is it? I think that is only a masculine view of the story's conflict. You could accurately describe the *Jaws* rip-offs as Man against Nature, as they had no characters of change—no armature. But *Jaws* has a solid armature. *Jaws* is about a man facing his fear and conquering it. I would say that is Man against Himself.

*Moby-Dick* has also been described by some as Man against Nature. This description totally ignores Captain Ahab's obsession with the white whale and how that obsession eventually kills him. The whale is only an external manifestation of Ahab's internal conflict.

There is no reason that the other two masculine conflicts

listed above can't include Man against Himself. In fact, to be full, they should. Otherwise, what's the point?

Things that affect a character physically are masculine and are visible ink. How he feels about them is feminine and invisible. If you can strike a balance between these two elements, your story stands a better chance of resonating with audiences.

Remember the masculine conflict only forces the hero to deal with his feminine conflict. It is the external pressure that makes a diamond of a lump of coal.

Look for ways to balance the masculine and feminine elements in your stories. More than likely, you will be drawn toward one over the other. Be careful of this; it will not serve you well to give into the things you already do well. If you go through the ritual pain of doing the very thing you don't want to do, you will become a better writer. You will ascend.

Just as the letter Y can sometimes be a vowel, theme can sometimes be a feminine element. In George Orwell's *Animal Farm*, the theme is the feminine element.

That story is a case where the characters must be stereotypes to represent the different strata of society. All components are there to illustrate the armature idea.

Writer Rod Serling used this kind of storytelling to great effect in his work on the classic *The Twilight Zone* television series.

In the 1960s and '70s, we learned a valuable lesson—that we should treat all people the same, regardless of race. But somewhere along the way we decided that what that meant was that we weren't to even notice, or acknowledge, a person's race.

As a black man, friends have sometimes told me that they never even noticed that I was black. We all know this is a lie. What they mean to say is that it doesn't matter to them that I'm black.

It is not a crime against society to notice that someone is different than you.

The crime is to judge them for it.

The differences between men and women have been used to keep women down. So we as a society have tried to fix things by pretending that we were all the same.

All the while being frustrated by the opposite sex and whispering in shadows with our friends that we just can't understand how men/women think.

Male brains and female brains are as different from one another as a ton of bricks is from a ton of feathers—equal but not the same.

I knew going into the idea of masculine and feminine traits was going to get me into trouble with some of you, so I did a little research on the subject.

I learned that the amount of testosterone we receive in the womb at a critical point in our development determines the "maleness" or "femaleness" of our brains. According to the book *Brain Sex* by Anne Moir, PhD, and David Jessel this has been accepted by virtually every brain specialist or neuroscientist. There are real physiological differences in the way our brains function.[1]

For instance, from the earliest ages, girls are more interested in interpersonal relationships than boys. Shortly after birth, girl babies show an interest in voices and faces, whereas boy babies show an interest in inanimate objects.

Throughout the animal kingdom, testosterone makes males more aggressive and competitive while female hormones decrease these traits.

Some of the traits enhanced by the testosterone-formed male brain are:

- a desire for status and power;
- an interest in how things work;
- an interest in acquiring facts and data;
- an emphasis on logic;
- an interest in problem solving;
- more aggressive than females;
- more competitive than females;
- and a more heightened sex drive than in females.

Female brains received less testosterone in the womb. Some of the traits enhanced in the female brain are:

- an interest in people;
- an interest in intimacy;
- an emphasis on interpersonal relationships;
- an interest in bonding with others;
- an interest in the feelings of others;
- and a greater ability to empathize.

It is easy to see why most men are drawn to a particular type of story given the inner workings of their brains.

Here, too, it is clearly seen why women are more often drawn to certain types of stories.

The corpus callosum is the link between the right and left hemispheres of the brain. In women, this connector is thicker, making it easier for women to exchange information between the two hemispheres.

Women store their emotions in both hemispheres while men keep their emotions only in the right hemisphere, making them more difficult to access. This explains why it is often said that men are not in touch with their emotions. They literally aren't. At least they are not as in touch as are women.

One study showed that when asked to identify the expressions on faces, women used very little of their brain to perform the task, whereas men used much more of their brain and had much more difficulty than women performing the task.

Not only are women more in touch with their own emotions than men, but they are more in touch with the feelings of others. Women are physiologically more equipped to empathize with others.

Whether you believe that these brain differences are a result of intelligent design or evolution, there must be a reason that each gender has a specialty. We must need both ways of seeing the world in order to survive in it.

Since I have been thinking about the masculine and feminine components of story construction, I've listened closely to the ways men and women talk about the films and books they enjoy. I was recently discussing a film with a friend of mine. She liked the film. I did not. What she said in the film's defense was that it had to be good because it made her cry four times. A response I often hear from women.

I know another woman who will always say, "How could you not like that film— it's so romantic!" Or she will say, "But it was so beautiful."

On the other end of the spectrum, many of my male friends gush over martial arts films or special effects extravaganzas devoid of any emotional content, but full of action or killing. When you look at the makeup of our brains, these responses seem to make more sense.

Consider a film such as *Casablanca*, which balances both feminine and masculine components very well. A very romantic film, but I know just as many men as women who respond to the film. It has a solid plot that ties in closely with the humanistic elements of the story. Achieving this balance gives stories a resonance that helps one reach a broader audience.

*It's a Wonderful Life* has some of the most romantic scenes I have seen in any film. It also deals with George Bailey's inner emotional life of depression and disappointment. It also has a strong plot. That balance crosses gender and time. Virtually every classic has close to equal parts of male and female elements.

The Omaha Beach sequence of *Saving Private Ryan* was hailed by both audiences and critics as being one of the most realistic war depictions in the history of film. Was it the great special effects that made it so? I don't believe so. The sequence contained both masculine and feminine elements.

When the sequence opens, Tom Hanks is having tremors, an external indication of his inner emotional condition. Other men on the Higgins boats begin to vomit from seasickness and nervous tension.

Before one shot is fired, we are already an uneasy audience. There is a sense of dread.

When the boats hit the beach, the men are riddled with bullets. How many times have we seen people being killed on film? Why is it that these deaths seemed to affect us more than most? It's because we had sense of how these men felt before they died—their abject terror.

I know men who are usually energized by depictions of violence on screen, but who were mortified by these scenes of death.

In one shot, a soldier wanders back and forth in the mayhem, looking for his missing arm. In another, a man with his insides exposed cries out for his mother as he lies dying. Although full of action, this is no action film.

This film is "realistic" because it is honest about the emotional impact of violence as well as the physical. I have seen actual footage of D-Day with men falling down dead and it seems less real than in Ryan. Why? It's because it isn't a complete picture.

Seeing a man fall over dead without knowing anything about him has less impact. *Saving Private Ryan* gives one a sense of what it might have felt like to be there.

Here's a good way to think of it: If a good friend of yours says to you, "There was a really bad car accident on the freeway yesterday," you might have some interest. On the other hand, if she says, "I was in a really bad car accident yesterday," your interest is much greater.

The first statement is all masculine; the second contains both male and female components. It involves emotion because you care about the person in the story.

I don't like everything about James Cameron's *Titanic*, but he does in that film exactly what I did with the car wreck example. At the beginning of the film (in present day) he has a man explain, in all male terms, what happened to the ship after it hit the iceberg and how it sank. Later in the film we see characters we know going through the experience. We get a sense of what it might have felt like to be on that sinking ship.

Remember that the *facts* are not necessarily the *truth*. The cold fact that the Titanic sank says little about the truth of the experience.

You don't have to take my word for this idea of masculine and feminine story elements. Listen to how people talk about stories they read, watch, and write. They will more than likely fall in one camp or the other and downplay the importance of the opposite element. They will be all-plot-and-action or all-character-and-mood. This division will probably fall along gender lines. It's just the way our brains work.[2]

---

[1] Anne Moir, PhD, and David Jessel, *Brain Sex: The Real Difference Between Men and Women* (New York: Dell Publishing, 1992).

[2] There has been much scientific study on gender brain differences and there are a few books and articles on the subject worth taking a look at:

- *Why Men Don't Listen and Women Can't Read Maps: How We're Different and What to Do About It*, by Barbara Pease and Allan Pease. Broadway Books 2001.
- *Psychology Today* Jul/Aug 2003.
- *The Wonder of Boys*, by Michael Gurian, PhD, Penguin Group (USA) Inc. 1997.

## Drama in real life

In 1968, sparked by the assassination of Martin Luther King Jr., an elementary school teacher from the all-white town of Riceville, Iowa, tried an exercise to teach her young students about prejudice. The exercise became an annual event.

She first asked the kids what it meant to be prejudiced. They all knew what it meant, and that it was bad.

Then she told them that those of them with brown eyes were better than those with blue eyes. Using the tried-and-true stereotypes of racism, she said that blue-eyed people were lazy and stupid.

The blue-eyed kids were to be shunned for the entire school day. They were not to be played with or spoken to. They could not use the drinking fountain and were not allowed to use the playground equipment at recess.

In contrast, the brown-eyed kids were given second helpings at lunch and an extra five minutes of playtime at recess. They were, in every way, treated better than the blue-eyed kids.

Needless to say, the blue-eyed kids had an awful day. Their brown-eyed classmates made life hell for them. They resorted to name-calling and teasing of those who were, just the day before, their friends.

The next day, the teacher told the children that she had lied about brown-eyed people being better, and that the reverse was true.

The blue-eyed children, now believing they were superior, behaved as their brown-eyed counterparts had the day before.

At the end of the second day, she told her students why she had put them through this painful experience.

Now, when they were asked about prejudice, these children understood it, and the evils of it, intimately. These young people were transformed forever. When interviewed about the experience as adults, they say it was life changing. They also say it was worth the pain they went through.

The teacher had told them about how bad prejudice is, but apparently the telling lesson did not take. You can see how experiencing rather than telling is what transformed these children through ritual pain. Remember, drama is a way of getting across an intellectual idea emotionally. That is exactly what happened here.

When film of the elementary school teacher's exercise is shown to adults, they learn all of the lessons the kids did, but without having to go through the experience themselves.

This is what makes drama so powerful—it is a way for people to experience things without actually experiencing them.

Your responsibility as a storyteller is to be a good teacher, not a good preacher. If you only talk about what you want to say, you are only proselytizing. But if you show your audience through demonstration, it will learn, seemingly, on its own. Not only that, but its members will learn it more thoroughly.

This is why here, in this book, I use so many stories to make my points. I want you to make the observations yourself, with my guidance.

There is more to this remarkable story, by the way. The teacher, Jane Elliot, suffered greatly for her actions. She was called a "nigger-lover" and received death threats from angry parents and townspeople. Her own children became the targets of violence perpetrated by other kids.

Through all of this, she kept doing what she thought was right. She kept right on doing her exercise.

She made personal sacrifices for the greater good. This is the definition of a hero in life as well as drama.

Every element of drama has its real-life counterpart. Try to notice the invisible ink in life as well as fiction.

# The myth of genre

Genre is visible. People know if they are watching a western or science fiction. But invisible ink is about the inner workings of story, not the costumes the characters wear.

Among the people who know me, I am known as the guy who doesn't like any film that comes out. This isn't true; it's mostly true. Anyway, they rack their brains trying to figure out what it is I do like and why. They think it might be subject matter or a certain kind of tone or maybe a particular genre. But there is always some wild card film that blows their theory.

Among people I work with, I am known as a person who can go easily from writing one genre to another. They can't figure out how I do it. It's simple. I just try to tell a story and tell it well. That is the same thing I want from other storytellers as well.

I believe that thinking of stories in genre terms only makes one think of how stories are different from one another instead of what they all have in common. Good drama doesn't understand the boundaries of genre. It doesn't care if someone rides a horse, a car, or a spaceship, as long as you care about the rider.

Genre is concerned with the external. Some stories have been told in completely different genres with only cosmetic changes. Akira Kurosawa's *Hidden Fortress*, a samurai movie, became the basis for the first *Star Wars* film. Another Kurosawa film, *Seven Samurai*, became a western.

Kurosawa himself took William Shakespeare's *King Lear* and set it in feudal Japan. Patrick Stewart took that same story and set it in nineteenth-century Texas for his television production, *King of Texas*.

The classic musical *West Side Story* is *Romeo and Juliet* updated and set in the world of rival street gangs in 1950s New York.

The John Wayne western *Red River* is a retelling of the classic sea epic *Mutiny on the Bounty*. Same story, different genre.

Genre is irrelevant to the dramatist. A dramatist should only be concerned with drama. If one genre can help you tell your story better than another, use it. No genre is better or worse than another.

If you think about it, *Jaws* is just a monster movie. And, like a lot of monster movies, incidental characters are picked off as our hero tries to stop the creature. But somehow, the film transcends genre. It's because it has an armature and a character of change.

Lots of films came out after *Jaws* that tried to repeat its success by emulating its masculine elements. One film used an orca whale in place of a shark, and another used a mutated bear.

None of these films went below the surface to understand why *Jaws* had resonance.

*Terminator* and *Aliens* are also just monster movies on the outside; what sets them apart are their strong armatures.

This happens in literature as well. No one ever says that *1984* is just a science fiction novel. Or that *Animal Farm* is a kid's book because it has talking animals. Nor do they say the same of *Gulliver's Travels* because its world is fantastic.

Is *Star Wars* sci–fi or is it fantasy or is it action? If it is sci–fi, does it have anything in common with *Alien*? What do *E.T.* and *2001: A Space Odyssey* have in common? What are the similarities between *Terminator 2* and *Galaxy Quest*? Indeed there is little these films share in common.

We have also prescribed a hierarchy to genre stories: "This is a costume drama; it must have more to say than a sci–fi story." This, of course, is not the truth.

When Clint Eastwood made *Unforgiven*, it felt like few westerns before it because it was more concerned with theme than with props, setting, costumes, and stereotypes. It transcended genre.

Fed up with the restrictions enforced on him by networks and advertisers, Rod Serling stopped writing the prestigious teleplays for live television for which he was famous. When he announced that he would be doing a fantasy show, many thought he had given up on doing "serious work" for television.

Mr. Serling knew something the executives didn't. "I knew I could have Martians say things that Democrats and Republicans couldn't," he said. He was able to use the prejudice of genre hierarchy to his advantage.

He wrote fantastical stories about real human issues without any flack from advertisers, and audiences always knew what he was saying.

We all have a fondness for a particular motif. I like the clothes and cars from the mid-twentieth century. I have a visceral response to those things when I see them in movies. That doesn't make the film good.

More importantly, other people may not share my appreciation for these things, so as a storyteller, I must speak to them on a deeper level. The armature must be so strong that it makes the story universal and makes the genre inconsequential.

As a storyteller, you should be aware in which genre your story will, more than likely, be viewed. Outwardly, it should be in a recognized genre.

That will make it much easier to sell and to market. Only you need to know you've transcended the genre. Your audience will know it too; they just won't know they know.

Related to this topic is the idea that one medium is superior to another—live theater is more artistic than cinema—or that novels are inherently better than comic books. Or movies are better than television.

These are all just mediums that can be used to tell stories and that is all. Each has its own strengths, and it is up to you to use the strengths of whichever medium you choose to help tell your story.

If you want to test this idea, read the graphic novels (comic books) *Maus* and *Maus II*, by Art Spiegelman. It was the first comic book ever to win a Pulitzer Prize. A special category had to be created so that the book qualified.

Will Eisner's graphic novels are also worth your time. I'm sure that if he told stories in another medium, everyone would know his name. In fact, the top award in comics bears his name. He has won several, by the way.

Early in the days of movies, they were thought to have no importance, a cheap dirty little entertainment. Most "legitimate" actors avoided the "flickers" all together. But there were a few pioneers who saw the power of the medium and learned to use it to tell stories.

D. W. Griffith was the first filmmaker to use crosscutting; that is, cutting between one scene and another to build tension. When others voiced their concerns, saying that it might confuse the audience, he said, "If Dickens can do it, so can I."

Don't let your medium or your genre stop you from telling a good story.

## Climax

One of my students once asked me, "What about climax?" At first, I didn't understand the question. What about climax? I thought it was pretty self-explanatory. It's the one thing everyone knows about story structure—that at the end, there's a climax. But I thought about it more and realized: A climax is the bringing together of the masculine and feminine elements that shows the character's change, or lack thereof. We can see how much a character has changed based on how they respond when the pressure is on.

At the climax of *E.T.*, the government guys are after the alien, and Elliot helps him go home. Elliot does this even though it hurts him.

Going back to sacrifice, one of the things sacrifice does is allow audience members to see the sincerity of a character's change. It gives them a yardstick by which to measure growth.

In *Tootsie*, Dustin Hoffman could continue lying about being a woman, but at the climax he has grown enough to tell the truth. At the climax, he reveals himself to be a man on live television. He does this despite the possibility of a lawsuit by his employers and the alienation of the woman he has fallen in love with. But he is an honest man now, and we see it through his extreme actions.

In *Casablanca*, Bogart does precisely what he said he wouldn't do and he "sticks his neck out" for others by killing a man and giving up the woman he loves. Nothing forces him to do this except his own growth.

In *Jaws*, the climax occurs when the protagonist is alone on a sinking boat as the shark makes its way toward him. But he has the courage to do what he does. His fear is gone.

The climax of *The Twilight Zone*, mentioned earlier, is when the man having the birthday challenges the others to kill the kid with the powers. He makes a sacrifice, but since the others don't respond to his call, it is for nothing. But we can measure their lack of change by their inaction.

The climax of the play A Doll's House is Nora's change. She stands up to her husband in a way she never would have at the beginning of the play.

Simply put, the climax of a story puts the protagonist in an intense situation that forces a choice that shows growth or lack of growth.

This is only true of stories that transcend genre and have a solid armature.

## God from the machine

You may have noticed in a cartoon or two that, often, when Bugs Bunny is in trouble, he reaches into a pocket and pulls out exactly what he needs. Not only does he have what he needs, but he doesn't even have a pocket until he needs one. This is called deus ex machina. It translates to "God from the machine."

Ancient Greek playwrights would sometimes put a hero into a sticky situation, only to have him saved at the end by one of the Gods. The "God" would be lowered down to the stage, suspended by ropes or some such contraption or machine. This is where we get "God from the machine."

Guess what? Audiences got tired of this trick very fast. It's not very satisfying to have your hero not save himself. It's a cheat and it's lazy. It is a form of dishonesty and your job is to tell the truth, remember?

Sure, it works when Bugs Bunny does it, because it is so ridiculous it's funny. But most of the time, even in comedy, it is better to let your hero solve the problem—no invisible pockets.

On the other hand, if you want to spring a new problem on the audience, feel free. This works well because it only gets your character deeper into trouble. Trouble is good, because trouble is conflict, and conflict is ritual pain.

## Supporting plots (subplots)

I don't like the term subplot; I think it confuses people. What happens is that storytellers try to include subplots to flesh out their world and make it feel full. This is never a reason to introduce a character or subordinate (sub) plot.

I like to call them supporting plots. They are there to support the main plot. Everything should hang off the same armature.

Often, the story of the protagonist's clone will be seen as a subplot, but it only exists to help make your point—like the other "stalkers" in *There's Something About Mary*. Those are supporting plots.

The other womanizers in *Tootsie* only exist to put pressure on Hoffman's character to see himself in another light and change. How is that subordinate to the main plot? It isn't.

What about the man who honestly falls in love with Hoffman as a woman? It shows Hoffman how his lies can hurt people deeply.

There is nothing subordinate about these plots. I think that if you think of them as supporting plots, it will lead you down a path that supports what you are trying to say. Your world will, indeed, be fleshed out, but with things that matter.

Few can see the impact of supporting plots on the armature idea; but there they are, invisibly making stories more resonant.

## Slave, not master

I often have spoken to writers who say the reason they like writing is that
they have so much power. If you want it to snow, you can make it snow.
Or if you want to make it sunny, you can make it sunny. You can do
whatever you want. You are a master of the universe. Guess what—that is
not so. You are a slave to your story, not a master. Your characters, places,
scenes, and sequences must be built around the armature.

In *Raising Arizona*, when the convict escapes from prison, it is
raining. Why is this? It is because that scene has to resemble a birth as
much as possible. The mud dripping down the convict's face as he emerges
from the hole, screaming, helps complete the image of a grotesque birth.
The rain provides the mud, of course, but there is also thunder and
lightning. There is a storm, which further signifies something is wrong.

Think of it more as making discoveries rather than decisions. You
will then find yourself looking for things that illustrate your point. If you
do this, your work will be stronger and more focused. It will elevate your
work over most.

I know some storytellers who think they can buck the system.
They want to bend the rules of story around what they want to do. It
doesn't work. But they never seem to understand why people don't like
their work. It's a pretty simple rule—if you write without a destination,
it's a sure bet that you'll never get there.

| Chapter VI |

Dialogue

Sounding natural

Address and dismiss

Address and explain

## Dialogue

My barber wants to make a film. He wants to write a screenplay, so he wants to know the format. He figures that once he knows the format, he's set. There is nothing else to know, right? As he said to me, "I already know what I want people to say."

Most people are under the impression that scriptwriting is coming up with dialogue. Most critics seem to think this as well. They will go on and on about dialogue, but they know nothing about drama, or how it is structured.

I feel like dialogue is talked about and written about far too often. It is the writing that people can see, so they focus on it. Of course, you know now how much more there is to story construction. But I suppose I must write a little about dialogue.

Remember that invisible ink is the writing below the surface of the words. This invisible ink keeps the audience's brains active. Subtext is a kind of invisible ink. The dialogue exchange that follows is something I heard at a friend's house, over a Christmas breakfast, between a mother and her grown daughter.

```
                    MOTHER
          You sound hoarse.


                   DAUGHTER
          Yeah, I had a cold. It's going away,
          now.


                    MOTHER
          You should take care of that. How
          long have you had it?


                   DAUGHTER
          I'm fine. It hung on for a while. I'm
          fine.
```

                    MOTHER
        It's going away? You taking anything
        for it?


                   DAUGHTER
        I'm okay.

There is nothing unusual about this conversation. But here's the thing: The daughter's husband had recently died of AIDS. The daughter also had AIDS, but was not yet showing any signs of the disease. Read the exchange again with that in mind. That's subtext. That's invisible ink. Lots is being said, but not spoken.

Subtext is all in the setup. Once you establish that two characters hate each other, for instance, all you need to do is put them in the same room together and have them talk about the weather—the audience will do most of your work for you.

Dialogue is a tool, and just like any tool, you use it when you need it. It can be used to define your armature, give essential plot information, or reveal character. If it isn't doing that it isn't doing anything.

The following scene is from *Some Like it Hot*. In this scene, we meet the two main characters. They are musicians who play in a speakeasy during Prohibition.

**SOME LIKE IT HOT**
Screenplay by
Billy Wilder and I.A.L. Diamond 1958

*The girls have gone into a tap-dance. The captain of the chorus looks toward the bandstand, grins and winks at—JOE, the saxophone player. He winks back. JERRY, who is thumping the bass fiddle behind him, leans forward and taps Joe on the shoulder.*

> JERRY
>
> Say, Joe—tonight's the night, isn't it?

> JOE
>
> (eye on tap-dancer) I'll say.

> JERRY
>
> I mean, we get paid tonight, don't we?

> JOE
>
> Yeah. Why?

*He takes the mouthpiece out of his saxophone, wets the reed.*

> JERRY
>
> Because I lost a filling in my back tooth. I gotta go to the dentist tomorrow.

> JOE
>
> Dentist? We been out of work for four months—and you want to blow your first week's pay on your teeth?

> JERRY
>
> It's just a little inlay—it doesn't even have to be gold—

> JOE
>
> How can you be so selfish? We owe back rent— we're in for eighty-nine

```
                    JOE (CONT'D)
bucks to Moe's Delicatessen—we're
being sued by three Chinese lawyers
because our check bounced at the
laundry—we've borrowed money from
every girl in the line—


                    JERRY
You're right, Joe.


                    JOE
Of course I am.
```

This is called *exposition*. The scene gives us information about the financial status of these men, as well as about their personalities.

Exposition is some of the hardest writing to do. Finding a natural way to have characters speak things they already know can seem impossible at times. It is easy to do it clumsily. This *is* the *kind* of thing you should learn from observing the way others do it.

But here is a word of warning: now that you know what to look for, many of these techniques will seem obvious to you; be careful not to dismiss something because you can now see it.

## Sounding natural

Over the last few years, I have noticed that every character I read, or see in the movies or on television, sounds like characters in another movie or television show. Real people don't talk like movie people. Listen to how people speak. They didn't all grow up in your neighborhood, nor do they all have your educational background.

Because I've worked in both animation and comic books, I know a lot of illustrators. One of the things I learned is that the good ones always do life-drawings. They learn to draw the human figure from looking at a human figure. Sounds obvious, huh? Well it's not. Many comic book artists learn from copying other artists. These people are never as good draftsmen as their life-drawing counterparts. They will often hear the advice, "Draw from life." This is good advice for us all.

When you write dialogue, or anything else, think of yourself as a puppeteer. You are hiding under the table; you don't want anyone to be thinking of you. You want their attention on the puppet. Once they are thinking of you, you've lost them.

This does not mean you can't have a character say witty, funny, smart, profound things, but it had better be the character talking, not you.

As a storyteller, your job is to get out of the way of the story. This isn't about you. It may be about what you have to say, but it isn't about you. Let go of your ego.

## Address and dismiss

The first time I noticed this technique, I was watching John Carpenter's *The Thing*. In the film, an alien creature with the ability to assume any form terrorizes a group of men in an isolated research base.

In this particular scene, the alien has assumed the shape of one of the men, but then begins to distort. The neck stretches impossibly and tendons snap. The head detaches from the rest of the body as the other men watch in disbelief. The head, now upside down on the floor, sprouts spider's legs and grows two antennas with eyes on the ends. Even for this film, it was almost too much. They had reached the outer bounds of their reality. Just then one of the men says, "You gotta be fucking kidding."

This kind of dialogue can save you when you think you may lose your audience. Sometimes audience members need a representative within the narrative. It allows you to address and dismiss their concerns so that they can stay engrossed in the story.

A very famous address and dismiss is in *Butch Cassidy and the Sundance Kid*, when they are trying to escape the super-posse by jumping off a cliff into a river.

When Sundance admits he can't swim, Butch laughs and says, "Well, hell, the fall will probably kill you!"

This example cuts the audience off at the pass, so to speak, before they can say, "Give me a break, there is no way they could make that jump!"

In *Tootsie*, we must believe that the other characters believe Dustin Hoffman is a woman. There are many comments made by other characters about how unattractive Tootsie is. This is an excellent use of address and dismiss.

All of these examples get laughs from the audience. I think it's because it's another kind of truth-telling. It's a tricky tool because it could pull people out of the scene. It is a kind of wink to the audience that lets them know the storyteller knows that maybe she's gone too far; but when used correctly, it is seamless—invisible.

## Address and explain

This is related to address and dismiss but serves a different function. The best example is in the first *Star Wars*, when Luke Skywalker sees the Millennium Falcon for the first time. After it was revealed, a hush came over the audience as they took in the magnificent ship. Then Luke exclaims, "What a piece of junk!"

The crowed erupted with laughter, because that's not at all what we were thinking.

This was George Lucas's world and we knew nothing about it. There is no way we would have known that the ship was considered a piece of junk without that clever bit of dialogue.

One of the things that drives me crazy when people talk about "good dialogue" is that they never talk about how well it's used, only how it stood out. Some of the best dialogue is quiet and subtle and reveals things about plot, theme, or character, with the precision of a surgeon. Sometimes that means it's not quotable, but quotable dialogue is not the primary job of a storyteller.

| Chapter VII |

## Superior position

### Show them once so they know

## Superior position

> *There is a distinct difference between 'suspense' and 'surprise,' and yet many pictures continually confuse the two. I'll explain what I mean. We are now having a very innocent little chat. Let's suppose that there is a bomb underneath this table between us. Nothing happens, and then all of a sudden, 'Boom!' There is an explosion. The public is surprised, but prior to this surprise, it has seen an absolutely ordinary scene, of no special consequence. Now, let us take a suspense situation. The bomb is underneath the table and the public knows it, probably because they have seen the anarchist place it there.*
>
> *The public is aware the bomb is going to explode at one o'clock and there is a clock in the decor. The public can see that it is a quarter to one. In these conditions, the same innocuous conversation becomes fascinating because the public is participating in the scene. The audience is longing to warn the characters on the screen: 'You shouldn't be talking about such trivial matters. There is a bomb beneath you and it is about to explode!' In the first case we have given the public fifteen seconds of surprise at the moment of the explosion. In the second we have provided them with fifteen minutes of suspense. The conclusion is that whenever possible the public must be informed. Except when the surprise is a twist, that is, when the unexpected ending is, in itself, the highlight of the story.*

—Alfred Hitchcock

Alfred Hitchcock's definition of superior position is about the best there is. It is when the audience knows something that the characters do not know. Most of the time it's used for suspense, but not always.

In Chuck Jones's hilarious animated cartoon "Feed the Kitty", a huge bulldog adopts a sweet little kitten. The problem, or conflict, is that the woman of the house has forbidden the dog from bringing anything into the house, so he must keep his new pet a secret.

At one point in the film, the woman starts to make cookies, and unbeknownst to her, the kitten climbs into a bowl of batter set under an electric mixer. When the woman flicks the switch to mix the cookies she finds that her dog has pulled the plug. She doesn't know he's trying to save his pet and just thinks he's causing trouble. She puts the dog outside so that she can work uninterrupted. While the woman is putting the dog out, the kitten climbs out of the bowl and wanders off.

This all happens when no one is watching—except the audience. We now have superior position.

The woman returns to her cookies unaware there was ever a cat in her mix. Worried about his pet, the dog is outside looking through the window as the woman flips the mixer on. He is mortified as the beaters go to work on the batter and, he thinks, his little kitten.

I have seen this film in a movie theater and I have rarely heard such uproarious laughter than during this scene. The poor bulldog looks on in abject horror as the cookie dough is rolled out with a rolling pin, then cut by cookie-cutters, then put into an oven to bake.

Outside, the dog is a wreck. He blubbers like a baby and lies in a pool of his own tears.

Why is this so damned funny to an audience? And believe me it is funny.

It's funny because we know the cat is okay. Imagine how people would react if they thought the cute little kitten had been beaten, cut up, and baked. It wouldn't be very funny. But just letting the audience in on the joke allowed the storytellers to put that poor dog through hell.

Even frightening experiences in our own lives can be funny in the retelling because we have a superior position over our past selves. We know everything turned out okay.

Remember that you have this tool, and it can frighten or amuse an audience depending on how you apply it.

This kind of invisible ink is often overlooked by storytellers, but if you want to keep readers turning pages, or viewers watching, you would do well to master this technique.

Alfred Hitchcock used it to engage filmgoers throughout his fifty-year career.

## Show them once so they know

This is a great tool for storytelling. It is almost always invisible to an audience.

In the film *The African Queen*, there is a sequence in which their small boat is trapped on a sandbar. Humphrey Bogart's character must get into the river and try to pull the boat free by hand. Unable to free the boat, he climbs back aboard. When Katharine Hepburn notices that Bogart has leeches on him, Bogart goes into a panic. He is deathly afraid of, and disgusted by, leeches, and he trembles in horror. He is truly shaken by this event.

Shortly after the leeches have been removed, the characters realize there is nothing they can do to free the boat by staying aboard. So Bogart must try again to free it by hand. It means he must get back into the river. You can almost feel his dread as this realization sinks in.

When he starts down into the river we know how brave he is. We know that he's facing an obstacle that is particularly large for him. It is almost like he is his own clone character. We can measure his bravery next to his fear seen before.

This kind of invisible ink can be used a couple of ways.

*Close Encounters of the Third Kind* is a film that makes use of UFOs as part of its reality. Here is a famous scene from that film.

Richard Dreyfuss is in his truck at night and he is lost. He stops his car in the middle of the road to check his map. Behind him, we see a pair of headlights drive up. Dreyfuss waves the car around. The driver goes around Dreyfuss's truck.

Very shortly after, the scene is repeated almost exactly. Dreyfuss is stopped and looking at his map when a pair of headlights drives up. Without looking up from his map, Dreyfuss waves the car around. Unbeknownst to him the lights behind the truck rise vertically. (Good use of superior position, by the way.) It's a creepy scene.

It works so well because we saw the previous headlights behave in a normal fashion, so now we have a comparison for what is normal and what is strange. Very smart storytelling.

The interesting thing is that most people forget about the first set of headlights altogether, but it is what makes the second pair of lights strange and fantastic.

Spielberg does the same thing in the first *Jurassic Park* movie.

Knowing that the Tyrannosaurus rex's vision is based on motion, the Sam Neil character throws a road flare off into the distance so that the *T. rex* will follow the flare away from kids it's attempting to eat. It works.

Shortly after this, Jeff Goldblum's character tries the same thing. He waves the flare to get the dinosaur's attention. The *T. rex* chases Goldblum. Then Goldblum throws the flare off to the side expecting the monster to follow—it does not. It never misses a step and continues after Goldblum.

This creates a tension in the audience because we know what was supposed to happen and how it went wrong.

They use this kind of invisible ink in Pixar's *Finding Nemo.* The tough fish has a plan to escape the tank where they are kept. As he tells the other fish his plan, the filmmakers show us exactly how the plan is supposed to work, so that when it later goes wrong the audience knows where and how the plan derails.

This creates a kind of wonderful anxiety in the audience members. They bite their collective nails as they follow along and the plan is carried out. Will it work?

When I was a kid, I read a lot of magazines and books about special effects, and whenever they showed a photo of a miniature they would place a quarter or some such object next to it so the reader would have a sense of scale. One could see just how small the model was because we all know the size of a quarter.

This is akin to how the first two pigs are used in "The Three Little Pigs" story. As I said earlier, it is the failure of the first two pigs that allows us to measure the success of the third. In a sense, we have scale—things to compare.

We know how strange and unusual it is to have headlights float up instead of going around a car.

We feel that Jeff Goldblum is in real trouble with the *T. Rex* because his plan doesn't work as it should.

This form of invisible ink is often ignored by inexperienced story-crafters. They will often jump right to the third little pig expecting the audience will "get it." It won't.

Invisible ink is all about communicating with your audience clearly and getting it to feel and think what it needs to so it will experience your story.

| Chapter VIII |

**When bad things happen to good stories**

**How to translate critiques**

**Judging your own work**

## When bad things happen to good stories

One day I was watching *Close Encounters of the Third Kind* and I realized that it had the wrong ending. Who am I to say this? I'm just a guy who looked at the clues and saw the grammatical errors in the dramatic structure.

First, let me say that I like Spielberg. More than a few of you, I'm sure, don't like his work. But he is a master storyteller and you should learn all you can from him and use those skills to tell the stories you want to tell.

In short, *CE3K* is about a man, played by Richard Dreyfuss, who sees a UFO one night and becomes obsessed with seeing it again. The UFO has planted an image in his brain, and he is driven to find out what this shape means.

He begins acting so strangely that his wife takes his kids and leaves him.

When he realizes that the image in his head is Devil's Tower, in Wyoming, he goes through hell and high water to get there.

I'm leaving out some details, but when he gets to Devil's Tower, he gets to see the UFOs and is invited to leave with the aliens. This is what he's wanted, so he leaps at the chance and boards the spaceship. It flies into the sky over the closing credits, taking Richard Dreyfuss away on a wondrous journey to parts unknown.

The End. This is the wrong ending.

Richard Dreyfuss has a wife and kids he's leaving behind. He didn't make a sacrifice. What he does is selfish. He has not grown from this experience at all.

There are even several clones in the film that tell you that Dreyfuss may be gone for decades. There are people returning to earth who have been missing for years. Where are their families now? Their lives will be disrupted forever. Yet Dreyfuss goes.

He even sees how upset one character is because her son was taken away from her, even for a short time.

The ending would have been stronger if Dreyfuss had to watch as the spaceship disappears into the sky while he stayed behind.

That's just my opinion, right? No, it isn't. After I noticed this problem with the film, I heard Spielberg himself say that he would have chosen a different ending now.

When he wrote the script, he didn't have a family and now he does. He said that he would make a different decision now.

Spielberg was making the mistake I see a lot of writers make. He was having the character do what he himself would have done in a given situation without really looking at what needed to happen for the story.

You are the slave of your story, not its master. You don't make decisions, you make discoveries.

Let's use another Spielberg film that I love, *Raiders of the Lost Ark*. What could possibly be wrong with that?

A good friend and I have an ongoing argument about this film, but ultimately I think we agree. He doesn't understand how Indiana knows to close his eyes when the Ark of the Covenant is opened.

My argument is that he's been set up as an expert on the Ark, so it's no surprise that he knows what to do at the end.

First, let's look at something that could be seen as deus ex machina—the literal appearance of God from a box to save the day. The storytellers did a very clever thing: they planted God throughout the film, so it is not out of the blue when God shows up at the end.

When Marion first produces the headpiece to the Staff of Ra, the wind begins to blow. She is inside when this happens; yet the wind blows.

Later, when the old Egyptian man translates the markings on the headpiece, the wind blows even harder than before. Again we are inside, so wind is a little unusual.

Then it comes time to dig up the Ark. Storm clouds boil with thunder and lightning. This is real Old Testament God behavior. (By the way, there is no other use of weather in the film.)

God gets more blatant later when the Nazi's swastika is burned off the crate where the Ark is being kept. By this time, we have been primed for God's appearance, so we aren't pulled out of the story.

What's the big deal when God comes out of the box at the end? It comes down to Indy's character change.

When the film starts, it is established that Indiana Jones does not believe in God. By the end of the film, he seems to believe in the Almighty.

None of these evidences of God are for Indy's benefit, they are never shown to him, so his change comes out of thin air. That's the deus ex machina, his sudden change. That's why my friend wants to know how Indy knew what to do at the end.

Albert Brooks is a hilarious filmmaker, but sometimes he makes mistakes in his storytelling. In his film *Mother,* he plays a man whose marriage has just broken up, so he goes to live with his mother to find out why he can't relate to women. He and his mother don't get along, and he figures this is where all of his woman trouble stems from.

Here's the problem: Because Albert Brooks decides to live with his mother, the conflict feels forced. The two have great, hilarious disagreements. They drive each other crazy, but one is always aware that Albert could leave anytime he wants. This takes the edge off their comedic conflict. I kept asking myself, "Why doesn't he just leave?" It isn't honest. Tell the truth, remember?

Whenever there are characters who don't want to be together, the storyteller needs to find some glue that holds them together. In *The Odd Couple,* for instance, Oscar is afraid Felix will kill himself. So, as much as his friend drives him crazy, Oscar doesn't want him to die. Felix stays because he has no place else to go. These two things are the glue that binds them together.

*Mother* could have used more glue. Watch it and see if you don't agree.

*Stalag 17* is a Billy Wilder film that, even though I have it on DVD, I can't keep from watching when it comes on TV. And as much as I love Mr. Wilder's work, I think this film is flawed.

The story takes place in a German POW camp during the Second World War. The Americans imprisoned there think there is a German spy living among them, in their barracks. William Holden plays Sefton, the suspected traitor. He is a wonderfully gray character, and it is easy to see why the others suspect him.

But there are two characters who seem not to serve any real function. They are comic relief, but they too often pull the focus away from the main story. Few things these characters do support the main plot. They are the fat on what is otherwise a lean script.

I have shown this film to people hoping they would enjoy it, and for many these two characters ruin the film.

You may think that I watch films looking for these types of mistakes, but I don't. After a while these things will stick out to you like a sour note to a musician.

## How to translate critiques

The truth of the matter is that most people don't have the skills to articulate what is bothering them about a piece of writing. They will see everything through the lens of their tastes and their concept of drama. Rarely will they look at what you are attempting to do and be able to give unbiased advice about how to achieve it. Their comments will be subjective, not objective. Everyone who reads the work will say something different.

They will say things to make themselves sound learned. They will correct your spelling and comma placement. They will hate the main character, but never tell you it's because he's just like a guy who owes them money. They will see things that are not there and never ever see the invisible ink.

So how do you sift through all of this and get to the helpful stuff? You must learn to hear what they mean, not what they say. Listen to the music, not the lyrics.

But if they say they didn't like the ending, remember what Billy Wilder said, "If there is something wrong with the third act, it is really in the first act."

Here are some hints:

• If you hear the same critique from three or more people, listen to it. But keep in mind they might be describing the symptom, not the disease.

• If someone doesn't understand what is going on in your story, that is worth listening to.

• If someone loses interest in your story, it is worth finding out where.

• Other writers can often be the worst at giving critiques. They will try to remake you in their image. "This is how I would do it." Only they won't say that out loud.

• If you clearly communicate your story, other writers will often say that it's too blatant.

This is something I learned when I worked in animation. When you show work in progress, they will always feel obliged to tell you what's wrong with it and how to fix it. But when you show them a finished piece, they are much more accepting.

## Judging your own work

*A writer is someone for whom writing is more difficult than it is for other people.*
—Thomas Mann

Don't write for other writers. People are drawn to writing for different reasons and many people do it to seem smart. If you have a good first act, most will never recognize it, because they're not really clear on what a first act does. They know nothing of construction, but will turn their noses up at the idea of it anyway. The less they know about it the more they will object to it.

The one thing I have noticed about people who are exceptional in their creative work is that they are always trying to get better. That's how they got good in the first place. These people judge themselves against the best work. They aim for the top.

Just worry about the craft and the art will take care of itself.

The term self-expression has had a harmful impact on storytellers. Stories are not about the storyteller. If your focus is on yourself, then it is not on what is best for your story.

Learn to look at your work as if it isn't your work. Be as hard on yourself as you would anyone else.

Learn from the masters. Figure out how they did what they did, why it worked, and apply it.

Don't be fooled by flash-in-the-pan successes and don't try to imitate what is new and novel. If someone comes along and does something different, such as telling a story backwards, or out of sequence, it doesn't mean it's going to be the way things are done from now on. How many backward movies do you want to see?

Respect your audience. It's not their job to "get it"; it's your job to communicate it to them.

Understand that you are only as good as you are today, and don't beat yourself up. You'll get better.

| Chapter IX |

**Good stories, good business**

## Good stories, good business

In 1993, there were, as I understand it, more comic books published than in any other year. Just a few short years later, so few comics were selling that many wondered if the medium would even survive. Why the big turnaround? Lack of story and story-craft.

In the world of comic books, the superstars are the artists. Most fans are initially attracted to the artwork in a book. In the early '90s, editors started letting more of these popular illustrators write as well as draw.

Some of these artists broke from the major publishers and started to produce books of their own. Understandably, these new businesses wanted people to buy their product, so they touted and promoted each book as a collector's item. This worked amazingly well.

They put out books with alternate covers. They had gold covers, silver covers, platinum covers, and glow-in-the-dark covers. The idea was to sell as many copies of a single issue as possible. Some collectors would buy ten to twenty copies of a book. This plan seemed to be working like a charm.

After a while, the speculator market dried up. I suspect they started to realize what makes *Superman* #1 valuable is the fact that not everyone in the world has twenty copies. And that printing the words "Collector's Item" on the cover didn't necessarily make it so.

What was the flaw in their plan? They went after buyers, not readers. Few people were actually reading these comics. Why? Few of these new companies bothered to hire professional, skilled writers. If the artist was not writing the book, he hired an old buddy from high school to do it. These "writers" had no sense of craft and their bosses didn't care. After all, these books weren't for reading, they were for putting into plastic bags and storing in a safe place until the collector saw fit to sell them for a truckload of money.

Here's the thing: if they had tried to get people interested in the stories and characters, people may have kept buying these books, even when they realized that they wouldn't be worth a bunch of money.

These companies devalued the importance of story at their peril. Now most of these companies are gone, or are mere shadows of what they once were, and their comic books can be found in that purgatory of comicdom—the quarter bin. Now, just twenty-five cents buys you a "collector's item," although the printed cover price may say two dollars or more.

One of these companies put out a guide for aspiring comic-book creators. In the section on writing, they said this: "Each issue should have a simple story goal… the next step is filler." This is no exaggeration. This was virtually the entire chapter on writing stories.

These companies didn't have even a rudimentary understanding of how stories are constructed or of their purpose.

On the flip side of that same coin is this: When I was a kid, writer/artist Frank Miller was doing *Daredevil* for Marvel Comics, and I would read them in school. There was a girl in my math class who teased me for reading comics.

One day, she was bored, having finished her assignment, and asked if she could read one of my comics. I gave her an issue of *Daredevil*. She got caught up in the story and wanted to read more. I brought her the entire run of the series. She plowed through the books, and upon completing the last issue, requested the next. She was flabbergasted to hear she would have to wait an entire month!

Miller had crafted a book with a balance of masculine and feminine elements. There was plenty of action, but there was always an emotional component to what was happening that made me, the girl in my math class, and thousands of other people, wait with baited breath for each issue.

When Miller took over the storytelling chores on *Daredevil*, it went from being one of Marvel's least-selling books to one of its most popular. Marvel is still making money off Miller's run on the series two decades later.

I recently had drinks with a Hollywood agent at a major agency. We got into a little debate. He kept saying that good films are hard to make, otherwise everyone would be doing it. That sounds good, except I rarely meet practitioners of story who have bothered to do any real study of their craft. They try to reinvent the wheel every time. Or they use a formula that only concentrates on the masculine elements of the story because they perceive that is what audiences really respond to. Or they write something that only uses the feminine elements of the story and then curse the audience for not responding.

The fact is, some storytellers throughout history have been able to have repeated success during their lives, and their stories live beyond their own limited lifespans.

How is this possible? They must be using methods that allow them to speak deeply to a large group of people across culture and time. They were able to repeat their successes, and if you learn their techniques, you stand a better chance of doing so yourself.

In the summer of 2003, the studios were baffled when they released a slew of sequels and franchise films that made much less at the box-office than expected.

According to *The New York Times*: "*The Hulk*, director Ang Lee's eagerly anticipated version of that comic book saga, opened robustly on June 20 (a $62.1 million opening weekend), ticket sales plummeted 70 percent in its second weekend."

Another film expected to do well that summer was *Charlie's Angels: Full Throttle*.

Also, from that same *New York Times* article: "'The *Charlie's Angels* case is a fascinating one, because it had all the earmarks of being a phenomenal success,' said David Davis, an entertainment analyst for Houlihan, Lokey, Howard and Zukin, an investment banking firm. 'A very expensive marketing spend, all of the stars doing publicity—it had everything going for it. I don't know, maybe after so many of these kind of movies so many weekends in a row, it was just one weekend too many.'"

Most all of these summer films were a disappointment to the studios that made and released them and to the audiences that saw them. Notice how the analyst does not mention the quality of the film's story when he speculates on the film's poor reception.

That same summer, Pixar, once again, had a huge hit on their hands with *Finding Nemo.*

The good folks at Pixar are almost exclusively concerned with story. They will work on a scene for months only to throw it out if it doesn't enhance the story. And they have, at the time of my writing this, nothing but hit films under their belts. Further making my point, *Finding Nemo* went on to become the highest selling DVD of all time.

I have a friend who was in the story department of another production company. Their job was to come up with feature film ideas to be done using computer graphics. This was after *Shrek* had become a huge hit. My friend told me that he was told not to mention the *Toy Story* movies as a reference point in his story pitches to studios, because those were considered old. *Shrek* was what people wanted to see!

The thing that most people don't understand is that well-crafted stories never go out of style. One generation after another has been entertained by Walt Disney's version of *Snow White*—a film originally released in the 1930s.

The 1939 version of *The Wizard of Oz* still enthralls adults and children alike.

A film or book can be a hit for many reasons—timing, new technology, hip language. But only one thing makes a classic—a good story that speaks to the truth of being human.

This is not invisible ink; it is clear to see for anyone who bothers to look—telling good stories and telling them well can be good business as well as being good for the world that consumes them.

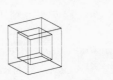

| Chapter X |

**My own process**

*White Face*

**Tell them what you told them**

## My own process

**F**ollowing is the screenplay for my short film *White Face*. When I set out to make this film, I was told by those in the know that short films do not make money. There are few venues for them. It got distribution, makes money, and shows no sign of slowing down.

Here's what I'd like you to do: Read the script twice. The first time, just read it without thinking too much about structure. Just get a feel for it. On the second read, see how much invisible ink you can find.

WHITE FACE
By
Brian McDonald

This Draft 10/27/99
©Angry Young Man Prod.

An *X-RAY* on a light-board. *TWO VOICES* off-screen
discuss the patient's condition. Their language
is highly technical and difficult to understand.
Fingers point out different areas of the x-ray.

PULL BACK TO REVEAL

INT. HOSPITAL-DAY.

*TWO DOCTORS in blue surgical scrubs. One of them
wears full CLOWN MAKE-UP, and a stethoscope
around his neck. As the two doctors continue to
confer with one another, none of the passers-
by seem to take notice that one of them is a
clown. Their talk is sober and; this is serious
business.*

             CLOWN DOCTOR (V.O.)
     I'm not going to sit here and tell you
     it was easy to get here.

EXT. HOSPITAL-LATER.

*The CLOWN DOCTOR sits on a bench outside the
hospital. He speaks to an off camera interviewer.
A caption reads:*
*Dr. Howard Blinky.*

             CLOWN DOCTOR (CONT'D)
     But I mean it's hard for everybody,
     right? I never thought being a clown
     would hold me back—I just didn't
     let it stand in my way. Sure there are
     the usual "Bozo" jokes. I've even

had patients refuse to let me
operate on them because I'm a
clown. That's true. That's
absolutely true. I remember this one
woman kept yelling: "Don't touch
me—get me a real Doctor." Can you
believe that? In this day and age.
> (beat; shrugs)
I'm good with kids though.

EXT. MECHANIC'S GARAGE-DAY.

*A MIDDLE-AGE CLOWN smokes a cigarette and
stands talking to the off-screen interviewer.
He wears a greasy jumpsuit and holds an
alternator. His caption reads: Ed Yuk-Yuk.
In the background another CLOWN MECHANIC is
working under the hood of a car.*

> ED YUK-YUK
> (New York accent)
Well I grew up in an all clown
neighborhood in the Bronx.

*INSERT: A photo of a New York residential
street in the '40s. Instead of "normal" people
the streets are populated by clowns.*

> ED YUK-YUK  (V.O.) (CONT'D)
I moved out here after I got out of
the Marine Corps. After Nam.

*INSERT: An old photo of Ed and his Marine
buddies.*

> ED YUK-YUK (V.O.) (CONT'D)
> Over there nobody cared if you were
> a clown or not. Every now and then
> some smart-ass would think it was
> funny to spray you with a seltzer
> bottle.

*Ed holds up his fist.*

> ED YUK-YUK
> Nobody ever did that crap more'n
> once.

INT. OLD CLOWN WOMAN'S HOUSE-DAY.
*The house is decorated with all types of CLOWN
FAMILY PHOTOS as well as Circus knick-knacks
and statuettes. The OLD CLOWN WOMAN walks out
of her kitchen with a cup of hot tea. She
talks to the off-screen interviewer.*

> OLD CLOWN WOMAN
> When my parents got here from the
> old country it was a real bad
> place for clowns. People would point
> at them and laugh everywhere they
> went. It was awful. Just awful.

*The woman sits. Her caption reads: Mrs.
Clarabelle Confetti.*

*INSERT: Old black and white film footage of
signs in windows: "NO CLOWNS ALLOWED" and
another which reads: "CLOWNS NEED NOT APPLY."*

                    CLARABELLE
You see in those days the only way
to get out of the old country was to
join the circus.  That's how our
people got associated with the
circus, don't you know.


INT. COLLEGE PROFESSOR'S OFFICE-DAY.
*This interview takes place in front of the*
*proverbial bookshelves. His caption reads:*
*Barnum N. Bailey Ph.D. Professor of Clown*
*studies. He talks over his half-glasses.*


                    PROF. BAILEY
So what you had happen around the
end of the nineteenth century is
that clowns became very popular
in entertainment. And, to cash in on
that, non-clown people began to put
on make-up to make themselves appear
to be clowns. They would have red
rubber noses that they could strap
on and they would perform in white-
face.


*INSERT: Old shot of clowns performing.*


                    PROF. BAILEY (V.O)
As these fake shows became more
popular the real Clowns were pushed
out of the business.


BACK TO PROF. BAILEY.

>               PROF. BAILEY
> There was so much prejudice at that
> time that audiences would rather pay
> to see someone pretending to be a
> clown rather than the real people.

*Depression footage of HOBO CLOWNS.*

>               PROF. BAILEY (V.O.)
> This is were we get the stereotype
> of the "Hobo Clown." "Hobo" is a
> very common name in the old country.
> In America, however, it has become a
> synonym for "Bum."

BACK TO PROF. BAILEY.

>               PROF. BAILEY (CONT'D)
> Well, really look at our entire
> language. Everything associated
> with being a clown has negative
> connotations. I dare anyone
> watching this show to go
> to work tomorrow morning and call
> their boss "a damn Clown" to
> his face.  Or call someone
> a Bozo—see if you don't
> get your lights turned out.

EXT. MIDDLE SCHOOL PARKING LOT-DAY.

*Dr. Blinky arms his car alarm with his key
chain remote and walks away from his BMW. The
camera follows close behind. Again the doctor
talks to the unseen interviewer.*

CLOWN DOCTOR
I got called away from the hospital—
my son got into another fight...kids.

INT. MIDDLE SCHOOL OFFICE-SHORTLY.

*The Doctor approaches the desk and talks to
the non- clown SECRETARY behind the desk.*

CLOWN DOCTOR
Yeah, I'm here about my son I'm—

SECRETARY (interrupts; nodding)
—Cameron's father. I could tell—he's
got your nose.

CLOWN DOCTOR
(sincere)
Really.

INT. PRINCIPAL'S OFFICE.
*Visibly upset the Doctor is led, by the non-
clown PRINCIPAL, into her office where CAMERON
is waiting. The young clown sits pouting in
a chair, his arms folded. The boy is dressed
like any other child his age.*

                    PRINCIPAL
I'm sorry I had to have you come
down here again—Cameron can't seem
to stay out of trouble.

*The Doctor lets out a nose-sigh and then*
*speaks to his son.*

                    DR. BLINKY
What happened?

*The boy shrugs.*

              DR. BLINKY (CONT'D)
Look, I can't leave work every time
you decide to get into a fight.
Now you are going to tell me what
happened. You know one more fight
and you're expelled.  Expelled.
You're not going to tell me again
that these boys are picking on
you for no reason—you must be doing
something.

              (to the Principal)
What happened?

                    PRINCIPAL
Well, you know how boys are.
He and two other boys were clowning
around—

   DR. BLINKY (interrupts)
—Whoa whoa wait a sec—I don't
appreciate that kind of—

PRINCIPAL
—I didn't mean it the way it
sounded. It's just an expression.
I thought that you people were
supposed to have a sense of humor.

DR. BLINKY
I don't care how you meant it.
Look, you know what, don't worry
about expelling him I'm taking
him out of here. Cameron get your
jacket.

*BACK IN THE PARKING LOT-SHORTLY.*

*Dr. Blinky stands next to his car angry and
upset. He is a little ashamed that the camera
has caught him in this very candid moment.
Massaging the bridge of his nose he holds back
his tears of frustration. After a few moments
he speaks. He looks up to reveal the TEARS
drawn on his face.*

DR. BLINKY
I'm sorry…I—I don't mean to cry…
it's just that you work hard all
your—I'm a Doctor for god's sake!
Do you have any idea how rare
that is—a Clown Doctor; even
in this day and age? I work
hard, damn hard, so my kids
won't have to go through
the same shi— crap. I can't
believe these attitudes still exist.
I went to Harvard!

*Cameron, now wearing his jacket, approaches the car. He also sports quite big floppy shoes. They can be heard slapping the pavement.*

INT. COLLEGE PROFESSOR'S OFFICE-DAY.

*Prof. Bailey addresses the interviewer.*

> PROF. BAILEY
> Many people erroneously believe
> that things have changed because
> of certain celebrity Clowns. And,
> indeed, some Clowns have done quite
> well for themselves—many
> by playing up offensive circus
> stereotypes. Ronald McDonald
> and Bozo for example. I
> honestly don't know how they sleep
> at night.

EXT. ED YUK-YUK'S-DAY.

*Near a car with its hood open the Clown mechanic is involved in a heated discussion with a customer.*

> CUSTOMER
> ...But how do I know they needed to be
> replaced?

> ED YUK-YUK
> You want to see your old parts—
> I can show you the old parts.
> (Calling to a Clown in the shop)
> Rollo, bring out the old parts.

                    CUSTOMER
I'm just saying I bring it in for a
tune up and you tell me it needs all
this extra work. How am I supposed
to—

                    ED YUK-YUK
—What extra work, we just replaced
the spark plugs. That's a normal
thing to do with a tune-up.

*ROLLO arrives with a shallow box containing
spark plugs and shows them to the customer,
who is a little embarrassed and tries to cover
up.*

                    CUSTOMER
Yeah, but how do I know that those
are my old plugs?

                    ED YUK-YUK (to Rollo)
Are those the man's plugs?

*Rollo answers not by talking but by HONKING
his BICYCLE HORN a few times. This is the last
straw for the customer.*

                    CUSTOMER
Great. This one doesn't even
speak English. I try to help you
people out, give you a little
business and you try and cheat me.

*The customer has been caught being a bigot on*

film, *so he explains his position right into the camera.*

> CUSTOMER (CONT'D)
> Look, I'm not prejudiced or anything
> it's just that if you're gonna
> come to this country I think
> you should learn to speak
> American. It's for their
> own good. Besides who
> knows what they're talking about.
> They could be talking about you
> right in front of your face and you
> wouldn't even know it.
>
> (Back to Ed)
> What do I owe you? I'm going to a
> real mechanic, one that at least
> speaks the language!

*The mechanic slams the car's hood shut.*

> ED YUK-YUK
> I don't want your money, why don't
> you just get the hell outta here
> before you find yourself pulling
> my size thirty-six shoes outta your
> ass.

*The man gets in his car and backs out into the street. Rollo is pissed off and he HONKS angrily at the car. The customer HONKS his CAR HORN back at Rollo as his car speeds away.*

EXT. ED YUK-YUK'S GARAGE-DAY.

*Rollo looks a little sad; he HONKS to the off-screen interviewer as subtitles translate for us. Ed stands next to his cousin; he listens and nods.*

ROLLO'S SUBTITLES
My cousin used to send me postcards
from America; it seemed like a
paradise. Home of Ronald
McDonald's, yes? But this America
is no place for Clowns—we cannot all
live in a castle with arches of gold
like Mr. McDonald's.

CLARABELLE'S HOUSE-DAY.

*She shows some old family photographs to the camera.*

CLARABELLE
...And these are my parents. Here's
one of my husband, Chuckles—God
rest his soul. Rodeo accident. It'll
be nine years in July. He
had the most beautiful smile.

*Her mood changes as she shows the next few photos. She's a little angry.*

CLARABELLE (CONT'D)
This is my son Bobo—he married
outside the race don't you know.

(Whispers, confidentially)
His wife is a Mime.

> (Normal voice)
> What made him go out and do something
> like that I don't know. Those people
> aren't like us—but it's his life.
> I'm just glad his father didn't
> live to see it. It's really the
> children that I feel sorry for.
> They won't know if they're Clowns
> or Mimes. Oh, and his wife, I can't
> understand one word that woman says.

*She mimics being trapped in a box—then suddenly concerned:*

> CLARABELLE (CONT'D)
> She's not going to see this is she?

EXT. PARK BENCH-DAY.

*Dr. Blinky sits on a park bench, enjoying an ice cream cone, with Cameron. There are no tears drawn on his face. He talks to the interviewer.*

> DR. BLINKY
> This thing with my son has really
> made me stop and take a long
> hard look at that man in
> the mirror. I thought that a good
> job, a Beamer and a house in the
> 'burbs was gonna fix everything. That
> people would see me as a person first
> and maybe just plain forget that I'm
> a Clown.

(laughs at himself)
I guess the world hasn't changed
much since I was a kid—people
still think it's funny to make fun
of someone who doesn't look like
them. Maybe things will be different
for my son's generation.

EXT. MECHANIC'S GARAGE-DAY.

*Ed the Mechanic Clown stands outside his shop
talking to the interviewer.*

                    MECHANIC CLOWN
I talked my cousin Rollo into staying
in this country. Sure it has it's
problems, but I still think it's
the best country in the world. Things
are getting better all the time for
Clowns. The way things are going it
looks like, one day, we might even
have a Clown in the White House.

INT. COLLEGE PROFESSOR'S OFFICE-DAY.

*Prof. Bailey addresses the interviewer.*

                    PROF. BAILEY
In the end it is incumbent upon
those Clowns in powerful positions to
educate people about our problems.
There are many Clown celebrities who
choose to remain "closeted," if you
will. These individuals are usually
of mixed heritage and with a little
make-up can "pass" so to speak for
another, more accepted, race.

                    PROF. BAILEY (CONT'D)
Perhaps some of you watching this film

PROF. BAILEY (CONT'D)
have some clowns in your family
tree. You need to stand up and say to
America that you are clowns and proud
of it!

DISSOLVE TO:

A *photo of Clarabelle Confetti against a black*
*background on the left hand side of the screen.*
*The following captions fade up, on the right*
*and side, in turn.*

CAPTIONS
This film is dedicated to the memory of Miss
Clarabelle Confetti who passed away shortly
after filming was completed.
She was well loved in her community and her
memorial was attended by over one
hundred Clowns.
They all arrived in one limousine.

FADE OUT:

When people see *White Face*, they often think it's improvised. Most of the time people enjoy the film, but the structure is invisible to them.

Let's go through the script so that you can see what I was doing.

Notice how I started with Doctor Blinky in a normal setting doing an important job. This is the story's reality. Though this is a comedy, it uses incongruity rather than blatant slapstick or parody for its humor. It is a satire.

Also, the voice-over helps start to define that he is of a "Clown race," not just a guy in clown make-up.

The doctor's personality is defined, too. He is a man determined to overcome any racism in the world through his professional excellence. Not to mention that it reveals racism in this fictional world, and that it will be dealt with in this film.

Ed Yuk-Yuk, the mechanic, is more of a blue-collar guy. This starts to let us see that Clowns occupy various strata of society. Also, creating this tough-guy Clown who has been to Vietnam again says that much of the humor in this story will come out of incongruity. Using 'Nam also grounds the piece in a kind of reality. It says that this is the real world as we know it, but as if Clowns were a race of people; so it reiterates the idea that this story deals with race issues.

Clarabelle Confetti gives us a third perspective on this world. She allows us to see the past prejudices inflicted on Clowns.

These three distinct characters give us what appears to be a cross-section of Clown-America.

The professor is more of a device than a character. He tells the audience things they need to know to understand the story. For instance, when he talks about the negative connotations of the word "Clown," the scene in the principal's office in which the phrase "clowning around" is used, follows it. Because of what comes before, we know how to view the insult.

Notice now that the next time we visit each of the characters, a problem is introduced. Conflict. In the case of the doctor, it is his being called into the principal's office of his son's school. The mechanic is confronted by the bigotry of a customer. And the old woman reveals her own prejudice.

It makes me laugh, when people see the film, that they always mention how the film really gets going when the doctor and the principal have their scene together. Of course, it's the first conflict in the film. Conflict keeps people interested. But act 2 only works because of act 1. Act 1 becomes the invisible ink that makes the rest of the film work.

The doctor is often regarded as the main character. It is because he's the character of change in the story. In the second act his belief system is challenged. It's more than just something funny happening.

Each of the characters has his/her three acts. The second act for the mechanic is when he has a run-in with the bigoted customer. Through his intro in act 1, we know that Ed Yuk-Yuk is an American who grew up in the Bronx and fought for his country. So we understand how deep the insult cuts when he is accused of cheating a customer.

With Clarabelle, the conflict is her own bigotry. She thinks it's her son's choice of a wife, but we know different. How do we know? We know this because we have established a reality in which racists are bad people whose hatred can hurt others. Never mind that most of us believe that this is true in life; what is important is that it is dramatized by the story.

Act 3 is tricky to see here in these stories because it appears to be a part of act 2.

With Doctor Blinky, the scene at his car where he cries and we see the reaction to his experience is act 3.

In the mechanic's story, Rollo, the horn-honking Clown, is a less defined character and is more the internal voice of Ed. Is this country everything he thought it would be? Ed's beliefs are challenged here. The scene with Rollo's speech is that story's act 3.

Clarabelle's death is a combination act 3 and dénouement ("Ever since that day"). How does her story resolve itself? She dies. What is her "Ever since that day?" She dies. And you can bet her racist attitudes remained with her the remainder of her life. She did not change.

Doctor Blinky's dénouement? We can see in his last scene how he has changed. He is not the same person he was at the story's start. He has grown through the ritual pain of being confronted with racist viewpoints he had spent years denying. His son is a clone; a view of the doctor's past. Seeing how these attitudes affect his son is what forces him to change.

The story has a three-act structure, but most people don't see that it's there. It is invisible to them. I had a producer from a major star's production company call me after he had seen the film. He wanted to know if I would be interested in working with them, but first he wanted to see something that would show that I understood narrative.

Understand he loved the movie. He said he thought it was brilliant, but he couldn't tell if I could tell a story. He knew nothing of invisible ink.

## Tell them what you told them

I wasn't sure how to end this book until I gave it to a friend to read and she told me that she enjoyed the book because she and I share the same taste in films. I knew then that I had failed to get my point across. This is not about personal taste.

The idea that one could view a story through the lens of objectivity is so foreign to some that they don't even know it is a possibility. But if you are to master this craft, that is what you must strive to do.

When you read a sentence and find a misspelled word or grammar mistake, do you think for an instant that it might just be your opinion? You probably don't. That's because you understand the language and its rules. When you are speaking with someone who has only rudimentary skills in your language, you can tell immediately, just as you will soon be able to do with the language of drama.

One of your tasks as a storyteller is to understand that the language of story has its own rules of grammar and syntax. If you were watching *The Wizard of Oz* and, in it, they decided the idea should be Dorothy's about how to get the apples from the trees; and then they had Tin Man come up with other plans; and at the end of the story, they said it was Scarecrow who had the brains all along—it would all be bad grammar. It would be a mistake, and you would know it.

Drama is a language, and its principles can be observed, learned, and executed. One way to master this skill is to try to understand what you respond to in a story. Ask yourself if you are having a personal reaction to something outside the story. If you abhor violence in stories and you read a book that has violence in it, ask yourself if it is there to support the story's armature.

Conversely, if you enjoy violence, ask yourself the same question. Is it necessary for the story to be told this way? If the story were *The Godfather* then the answer would be yes. If the story is *Toy Story*, then the answer is probably no.

Ask yourself this question about dialogue, costumes, scenery, photography, religion, language, personal philosophy, politics, a particular actor or actress, special effects, genre, music, and any other element that might find its way into a story. You will have strong feelings about some of these things and it will distort your view of a story.

I once had a student tell me that she hated *E. T.* because of the swearing. Most of us would be hard-pressed to remember any swearing in the film, but it was enough to ruin the film for her. Many of us do this kind of thing. We will love or hate something in a story for reasons outside the story itself.

We must take ourselves out of the equation if we are ever to learn to see and use story structure. This is not easy, but it is possible to do. To do this you may have to suffer the ritual pain of letting go of some of the things you hold dear. If you go to see films because of the special effects, you must not let them cloud your judgment about the quality of the piece. Ask yourself if the story has resonance for those who care little for effects, or photography, or your favorite actor. Does it have an armature and does every element in the story contribute to dramatizing that armature? To do this effectively, you may have to die as the writer you are in order to be reborn. When you do it, many things that are now muddy in your mind will become clear. You will ascend.

You will see the footprints in the grass.